Also by Francesco Alberoni

MOVEMENT AND INSTITUTION (1983)

FALLING IN LOVE

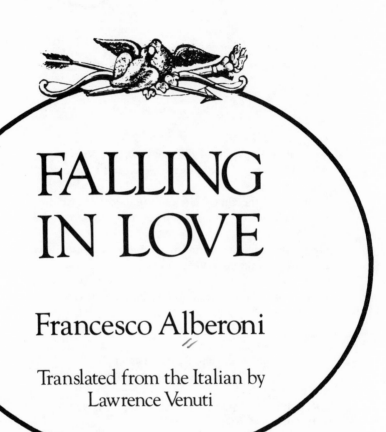

FALLING IN LOVE

Francesco Alberoni

Translated from the Italian by
Lawrence Venuti

Random House New York

Translation Copyright © 1983 by Lawrence Venuti
All rights reserved under International and Pan-American Copyright
Conventions.
Published in the United States by Random House, Inc., New York,
and simultaneously in Canada by Random House of Canada Limited,
Toronto.
Originally published in Italian as *Innamoramento e amore*
by Garzanti Editore. © Garzanti Editore s.p.a., 1981.

Library of Congress Cataloging in Publication Data

Alberoni, Francesco.
   Falling in love.

   Translation of: Innamoramento e amore.
   1. Love.   2. Change (Psychology)   3. Social change.
I. Title.
BF575.L8A413   1983   306.7'3   83-42757
ISBN 0-394-53007-1

First American Edition
9   8   7   6   5   4   3   2
Manufactured in the United States of America

FALLING IN LOVE

1

WHAT IS FALLING IN LOVE? *IT IS THE NASCENT STATE OF a collective movement involving two individuals.* This definition could have come at the end of a long discussion of facts and interpretations. I prefer to put it at the beginning, so that it may serve as our guide on this brief journey to a land that everyone knows, because we have all experienced it directly, but that remains so enigmatic and elusive. This definition poses the question of falling in love in a new way, according to a different perspective from the one handed down to us by psychology, sociology and art. Falling in love is not an everyday experience, a sublimation of sexuality or a caprice of the imagination. But neither is it a *sui generis* event, ineffable, divine or diabolic. It can be located in a class of phenomena that are already well known—the class of collective movements.* Among these, of course, it stands out unmistakably; it can't possibly be confused with other kinds of collective movements, such as the Protestant Reformation, the student movement, feminism, Davide Lazzaretti's move-

---

* On the general theoretical problem, see my study *Movement and Institution*, trans. Patricia Delmoro (New York: Columbia University Press, 1983).

ment,* or the Islamic movement of Khomeini. Yet falling in love belongs in this same class; it is a special instance of the collective movement. There is a very close relationship between the great collective movements of history and falling in love. The forces they both liberate and put to work are of the same type; they involve many similar experiences of solidarity, joy in life and renewal. The fundamental difference between them lies in the fact that the great collective movements are composed of large numbers of people and are open to still more. Falling in love, however, even though it is a collective movement, occurs only between two people. This restriction on its membership, whatever universal value it may have, is due to the fact that it is complete with only two people. This is the reason for its specificity, its singularity, the thing that gives it several unmistakable characteristics.

Many sociologists have already studied the collective movement and described the particular type of experience that it involves. Durkheim, for example, speaking of states of collective excitement, writes: "A man who experiences such sentiments feels himself dominated by outside forces that lead him and pervade his milieu. He feels himself in a world quite distinct from that of his own private existence. This is a world not only more intense but also qualitatively different. Following the collectivity, the in-

---

* Davide Lazzaretti (1834–1878) was a Tuscan carter turned preacher who proclaimed himself the second incarnation of Christ. He founded and led an ascetic penitential movement with millenarian beliefs. [Translator's note.]

dividual forgets himself for the common end and his con-
duct is orientated in terms of a standard outside himself.
... [These forces] need to overflow for the sake of over-
flowing, as in play without any specific objective.... At
such moments, this higher form of life is lived with such
intensity and exclusiveness that it monopolizes all minds
to the more or less complete exclusion of egoism and the
commonplace."* When he wrote these words, Durkheim
was not thinking at all about falling in love. He had in
mind the French Revolution and other great revolutionary events. In reality, the experience he describes is
much more widespread. It can be found not only in great
historical processes like the French Revolution and the
development of Christianity or Islam, but also in other,
smaller movements. Every collective movement in its initial phase, in what we shall later define as its nascent state,
has these characteristics. The curious fact is that Durkheim's words can also be applied to falling in love. Max
Weber has given us a second example in his study of the
phenomena that clearly demonstrate creativity, enthusiasm and faith. He looks at them, however, as a form of
power—that is, as something that depends on the emergence of a charismatic leader.† When this leader appears,
he breaks with tradition, leading his followers into a heroic adventure, and he produces in whoever follows him

* Emile Durkheim, "Value Judgments and Judgments of Reality,"
in *Sociology and Philosophy*, trans. D. F. Pocock (Chicago: Free Press,
1953), pp. 91–92.
† Max Weber, *Economy and Society*, ed. Guenther Roth and Claus
Wittich (Totowa, N.J.: Bedminster Press, 1968), vol. 3, chap. 14.

the experience of an interior rebirth, that radical change in outlook which Saint Paul terms "metanoia."

Under the charismatic leader's guide, economic concerns give way to the free unfolding of faith and the ideal, to a life of enthusiasm and passion. Weber attributes all these things to the leader, to his traits. In essence, he makes the same error that each one of us makes when we fall in love: we attribute the extraordinary experience we are having to the traits of the person we love. But the beloved isn't different from other people, just as we are not different from others. It is the kind of relationship established between us and the one we love, the kind of extraordinary experience we are undergoing, that transforms the beloved and, more profoundly, both lovers into something different and extraordinary.

Here, then, is our point of departure. In history, in social life, there are particular phenomena—collective movements—in which the relationships between people change substantially, radically, in which the quality of life and experience is transfigured. These moments signal the birth not only of religions—like Islam, Christianity, Protestantism—but also of sects, heresies and union or student movements. In brief, these are moments that signal the birth of a new collective "we" constructed out of two or more individuals, as when two people fall in love. In an existing social structure, the movement divides whoever was united and unites whoever was divided to form a new collective subject, a "we" which, in the case of falling in love, is formed by the lover-beloved couple. The forces that operate in both cases have the same violence and the same determination.

Until now, sociologists, psychologists and philosophers have felt some sort of repugnance or shame in admitting that great historical processes like the development of Islam and the French and Russian revolutions and private, everyday phenomena like falling in love may be somewhat similar, if not identical. A pride in greatness is involved here. These investigators wanted to concern themselves only with important, significant things—the central issues in social life. For them, the love between two ordinary middle-class people or two teen-agers, between an elementary-school teacher and a gardener, between a middle-aged man and his secretary, seemed so paltry, so dreary, so devoid of importance that it never occurred to them that the same forces they were studying might be at work in these passions.

A similar thing happened with the old biology. It was believed that first came man, the lord of creation made in the likeness of God; then the higher animals—the marvelous horse and lion; and at the very bottom, the worms, ants, mollusks. Today, however, we know that every animal has the same cellular structure, the same proteins making up its cells, the same DNA, the same synapses between its nerves. Of course, man and the higher animals are different, and we know very well how to distinguish a horse from a worm. But the difference derives from the fact that in the former the biological, biochemical and genetic mechanisms are basically integrated into much more complex systems. To understand things, we must study both shared and different mechanisms.

The experience of falling in love is the simplest form of collective movement; it can't be confused with the French

Revolution or the enthusiasm of the first Protestants. Nor is it true that a revolution is made up of the sum of many individuals falling in love, any more than a horse is made up of the sum of many worms, or that a horse is a very big worm. They are different things, but both are members of the same animal kingdom and are composed of the same fundamental elements.

The definition I began with—falling in love is the nascent state of a collective movement involving two individuals—has given us a theoretical field (a class) in which to situate that mysterious phenomenon: the field of collective movements. But the discovery that the experience of falling in love is a collective movement offers us, in turn, a formidable tool for investigating movements. These in fact appear only occasionally. A man may live his entire life without ever being involved in one, or he may be involved only once. Moreover, when we are dealing with thousands or millions of people, with all their economic and class interests, with every possible ideological variation, it becomes very difficult to study the elementary mechanisms. But falling in love is something that we all do: we can all vouch for our own experiences; we can tell our story, can speak. In this sense, the study of falling in love becomes the key to open the door to much more complex phenomena that may not happen in an individual's life.

But all this has no importance for our discussion; it is of interest to sociologists, philosophers and historians. We must now concern ourselves with one particular phenomenon, falling in love. To do so, we must immediately identify at least one of the distinctive characteristics of this experience. We must also dissociate ourselves from the current way of thinking which does not recognize falling in love as a state that is different from everyday life and sexuality. To avoid this view, which conceals the problem, let's begin with sexuality itself, while noting that here, too, there is a distinction between the ordinary and the extraordinary. Falling in love—like every collective movement—belongs in the realm of the extraordinary.

2

ACCORDING TO A WIDELY HELD VIEW, THE DIFFERENCE between human and animal sexuality lies in the fact that in animals sexual activity is cyclic—it appears explosively during the mating season and then disappears—but in man sexual desire is continuous, always present, and only fails to manifest itself with intensity if it is repressed. Sexuality is thus placed in the same class as other "needs," like sleeping or eating; it is always present in an almost constant quantity day after day. This idea spread with the popularization of psychoanalysis. In fact, Freud, in his quest for an original vital energy, initially identified it with sexuality. And while we are alive, the vital energy must exist constantly in us. Today this postulate is the basis for all those disquisitions on sexual misery as the effect of repression and domination which, beginning with the obscure reflections of Reich and Marcuse, have since come to animate the findings of countless public opinion surveys.*

What is repeatedly discovered in these surveys? That men and women have a limited number of rather brief

* Giampaolo Fabris and Rowena Davies, *Il mito del sesso* (Milan: Mondadori, 1978), p. 367.

sexual relations each week, and almost always with the same partner. So sexual activity is recurrent, short and of slight intensity, more or less like eating or drinking. The impression remains, however, that sex does not have to be like this, that it can be completely different. What is the source of this conviction?

It seems to me the answer is this: that all men and women have had periods in their lives when sexual activity was frequent, intense, extraordinary and exalting, and they would like it always to be this way. These extraordinary periods are taken as a standard for daily, ordinary sexuality, the kind that is measured in the public opinion surveys and that we experience almost habitually.

Now if we think carefully about the fact that we have all experienced brief periods of extraordinary sexuality and long periods of the ordinary kind, we will have to conclude that, in reality, human sexuality is not something constant like eating and drinking. Rather, it is always there in its *ordinary* form, like the other "needs," but it assumes a totally different, *extraordinary* form and intensity in certain periods—when we fall in love.

In man, sexuality does not have a biological cycle. In both man and animals, sexuality is discontinuous and is present in all its magnificence only during certain extraordinary periods, in love and in the mating season. At these times, sexuality is something inexhaustible and yet completely satisfying. We live for days on end, constantly absorbed in the person we love, and not only do we lose track of our sexual relations and their duration, but every glance, every touch, every thought addressed to her (or him) has an erotic intensity a hundred, a thousand times greater than that of ordinary sexual relations.

At these times, our entire physical and sensory life expands, becomes more intense; we pick up scents we didn't smell before, we perceive colors and lights we don't usually see. And our intellectual life expands too, so that we perceive relationships that were previously obscure to us. A gesture, a glance, a movement by the beloved speaks profoundly, tells us about her, her past, how she was as a child. We understand her sentiments, and we understand our own. We immediately sense what is sincere and what is not in others and in ourselves because we have become sincere. Yet we can create a universe of fantasies in which we never tire of rediscovering the one we love. And the erupting sexuality, the desire for pleasure and to give pleasure invests all that is part of her. We love everything about her, even the inside of her body, her liver, her lungs.

The sexual act then becomes a desire to be in the beloved's body, to live there and be experienced by her in a fusion that is physical, but that continues as tenderness for her weaknesses, her ingenuousness, her defects, her imperfections. We even manage to love a wound she might have, which is transfigured by our affection.

But all this is addressed to a single person and to her (or him) alone. In the end, it doesn't matter who the person may be; what matters is that along with our love a terrible force is born that leads to our fusion and makes each of us irreplaceable and unique for the other. The other, the beloved, becomes what only she can be, that absolutely special one. And this happens even against our will, even though we continue for a long time to believe that we can do without the one we love and can find that same happiness in another person.

But it isn't true. A brief separation is enough for us to reconfirm that the one we love is the bearer of something unmistakable, something that we always lack without her, that is revealed to us through her, and that without her we could never find again. And often we can simply identify her by a detail—her hands, the shape of her breasts, a crease in her flesh, her voice (it really doesn't matter what)—a detail that represents or symbolizes her difference and uniqueness. This is the "mark of grace." Eros—that is, extraordinary sexuality—is monogamous.

The facts, therefore, show us that our sexuality manifests itself in two ways, one of which is ordinary and daily, the other extraordinary and discontinuous. And the extraordinary occurs at particular moments: when we fall in love or when we experience a total, passionate love. *Ordinary sexuality*, like eating and drinking, accompanies us when our life proceeds uniformly, at the linear pace of the clock. *Extraordinary sexuality* appears at moments when our vital energy seeks new and different paths. At these times, sexuality becomes the means by which life explores the frontiers of the possible, the horizons of the imaginary and of nature: the nascent state.

This sexuality is tied to the intellect and the imagination, to enthusiasm and passion—it is fused with them. But its nature is to subvert, transform, rupture previous ties. Eros is a revolutionary force, even if limited to two people. And there are few revolutions in life. For this reason, extraordinary sexuality cannot be evoked at will. It signifies a vital change in us, or an attempt to change, and so it is risky. Eros is a source of constant aspiration and constant longing for us, yet we fear it. To protect ourselves we use the same word to indicate eros and everyday sexuality, the eating and drinking of sex, the subject of those public opinion surveys that always rediscover the same things. These are things that we already know, but that calm us because they tell us that other people experience the same "sexual misery"—that is, our everyday life.

But the surveys can also deceive us. They do so by suggesting that we can increase our happiness if, for example, we have sex ten times a week instead of four, if we increase the duration of each act, and, what is especially exciting, if we have sex with many different people. This is deceptive because when we are dealing with ordinary sexuality, having sex with the same person or with ninety-nine different persons doesn't change a thing. Anyone who has tried knows this, because he generally has tried it when he wanted to replace the one unique person who in herself could have given him satisfaction and peace during those intervals of time which, subjectively experienced, are moments of eternity.

Since we are used to measuring everything by the linear time of the clock, we forget that time is different in the extraordinary sexuality of true love. In Japanese Buddhism, the expressions *nin* and *ten* are used to indicate the two forms of the happy life. *Nin* is the world of peace and daily tranquillity, *ten* the extraordinary moment of emotion and love. Thus *nin* is already joy, and a day of *nin* corresponds to a year in a world without tranquillity. But a day of *ten* corresponds to a thousand or ten thousand years of time. In the nascent state there actually occurs an eternalization of the present. And when we lose our love, an hour's wait becomes years or centuries, and the nostalgia for the moment of eternity is always with us.

3

WHEN THE MOST SIMPLE AND UNAWARE PERSON FALLS in love, he (or she) is forced to use the language of poetry, religion and myth in order to express himself. This may seem amusing, but it is true. The reason is that religion and myth also spring from the extraordinary experience that is common to other movements—the *nascent state.* David's psalms, the mystical verse of Rumi and Dante, the poetry of Neruda and Quasimodo have different love objects. In Rumi the object is God; in Dante, a mystical transfiguration of a woman; in Neruda and Quasimodo, the fatherland, comrades, friends. Yet in all these cases the tone, hope, sense of destiny and ethos are the same. What is more, the Levellers' declaration of human rights can be put, without a single revision, in the mouths of two people who love one another but who have run up against an obstacle to their love. What we find, then, is the universal language of desire for something that is desired above every other thing, the universal language of liberation and right, the language of the triumphant life that creates a new ethos. What is established in every collective movement, and hence when we are in love, is established in opposition to customary interests and institutions, and to participate in this, to have the "right" to do so, we must enter a new region of values that have the same status as those interests and institutions. Falling in love challenges institutions on the level of their fundamental values. Its nature lies precisely in this, in not being a desire, a personal whim, but a movement that carries with it a plan for life and creates an institution.

Every collective process divides something that was united by tradition, habit and institutions, and unites something that was divided by them. When Christianity began, it separated Jews from their national religion and Roman citizens from the imperial cult and brought Jews and Gentiles together. Islam separated the Egyptians from the cult of their kings and the Persians from Zoroaster, and it united Arabs, Persians and Egyptians in a new way. Love too, when it appears in the history of the West, presents itself to us as laceration, separation. Ancient tribal communities, as well as agricultural and feudal societies, were founded on the structure of kinship. As Lévi-Strauss has shown, the kinship system is one of difference and exchange. A tribe, phratry or clan gives a woman to another clan and receives another woman in exchange. The couple is the result produced by the relationships within this structure. The choice of a wife is a transaction between two clans and in general is made directly by them. Or it may be made by individuals, but they must be members of a certain clan and only that one. In the feudal world, the transaction occurred between feudal families and only between certain families. But with the decline of feudalism, with the development of the bourgeoisie and hence of the possibility of accumulating wealth and achieving success, with the dissemination of culture and hence of prestige, these rigid bonds weakened, and it became possible to explore other paths. Let us be quite clear about this: the rules of the kinship system still existed; to violate them meant to commit a transgression and be punished. But while it was previously impossible to imagine leaving the system, one could now think of doing so.

The conditions that underlie collective movements are always these: on the one hand, we have a system of rules and institutions that continue to exist, while on the other, transformations proceed in society, and new classes, new powers and new possibilities arise. This is also true for falling in love. In feudal society, where the structure of kinship relations continued to exist even while a new bourgeoisie and a new intelligentsia were born, love struck like a spark between two individuals who belonged to two separate and noncommunicating systems. They sought out one another and united, transgressing the endogamic rules of the kinship and class systems. This was the case with Abélard and Héloïse. Their love was a transgression that asserted itself as exemplary and right, as a value. Of course, the love between Abélard and Héloïse was sexual passion, but what makes it love is not the fact that it was sexual, but that this sexuality, love, passion, pleasure presented and affirmed itself as the right to establish a relationship that conflicted with kinship and class rules. Abélard and Héloïse were married, but it was their love that gave legitimacy to their marriage. When Shakespeare, centuries later, represents Romeo and Juliet's love, he shows us an analogous situation: two hostile families between which marriage is prohibited. In this case, too, love presents itself as transgression. It separates what was united (Juliet from her family, Romeo from his) and unites what was divided (two enemies). No movement exists without a difference, and no experience of falling in love exists without the transgression of a difference. These may be any difference and any transgression; neither is fixed. Case by case, what separates and is transgressed is always different. It can be the simple fact that the boy is emotionally tied to his mother (or to his father), as in the modern world, and here the transgression is completely interior: the adolescent's rupture with the family of his childhood. For hundreds and hundreds of years, falling in love was presented as a rupture of the conjugal couple: adultery. But adultery is only a particular instance of a general rule: falling in love can occur only if it separates what was united and unites what needed to be divided. In terms of Lévi-Strauss's structuralism, love establishes another system of difference and exchange. At this point, we can better understand the limitations of what Denis de Rougemont has written.* He said that in the West, falling in love always presents itself as a prohibited, obstructed love. In reality, these obstacles are desired, wished for. The lovers, he maintains, don't really love one another; they derive pleasure from being apart. They are happy only when they are longing for the impossible. It really is true that in literature love is repre-

* Denis de Rougemont, *Love in the Western World*, trans. Montgomery Belgion (New York: Pantheon Books, 1956).

sented as obstructed or impossible (Dante, Petrarch, Shakespeare, Goethe and so on), but the explanation probably lies in this: if there is no obstacle, there can be no movement and therefore no falling in love. In other words, without the difference, without the obstacle, there is no need to establish another system of difference and exchange, to found another institution. In the fiction of literature, the obstacle is a device used to construct a love story endowed with meaning. In order to represent this situation, art creates imaginary obstacles: the hostile families in Shakespeare, Iseult's marriage, the birth of the new son in Goethe's *Elective Affinities*, Beatrice's death in Dante and so forth.

We shall see later that this artistic fiction serves to introduce two other essential elements of collective movements and hence of falling in love: the dilemma and, even more profound, the problem of perpetuating the nascent state. But at this point in our discussion we can content ourselves with the conclusion that what counts is not a particular kind of barrier, but the mere existence of a barrier. If at one time the barrier was represented by the kinship system, it may later be constituted by a previous marriage, a political belief, a cultural or linguistic difference, a difference in age or even a sexual difference, as in the case of homosexual love. Thus falling in love always consists of constructing something new, starting with two separated structures.

Let us now take a step back. Before an individual fell in love, what relationship existed between him and his family, his class, his church, his spouse, his ethnic or linguistic group? In other words, what relationship will he sever when he falls in love? We can assume that at first there was a pleasurable or at least an acceptable relationship, judged to be normal, legitimate. Of course, in all human relationships, no matter what kind they may be, there is always a more or less ample margin of dissatisfaction and disappointment; there is always ambivalence. The child in a family loves his father and mother, his brothers and sisters, even the family as a whole. The family is a collective object of love. Yet the family is also the locus of tensions and frustrations, of resentment and aggression. It is an object of love, but also of aggression: hence the ambivalence. Freud based his psychology on ambivalence: the Oedipus complex is the manifestation of ambivalence toward the father and the mother, who are loved, certainly, but also hated. Yet this hatred and rancor are not openly manifested. Even if there is ambivalence, the image of father, mother and family remains positive. And this happens because we feel the desire (we would probably have to say "the necessity") to preserve the object of our love in a state that is as pure and uncontaminated (unambivalent) as possible. The image that the child constructs of his mother and father, the image that the adult constructs of his church and political party, is the most perfect image possible. And he does everything he can to keep it perfect in his own eyes. To succeed in this, he learns, on the one hand, to take out his aggression on himself and express it as a sense of guilt (depression) and, on the other, to explain the imperfection he sees by attributing it to an enemy. The father is angry because he works too hard;

the nation or party or church is imperfect because inside or outside of it there exist enemies, wicked people (persecution). Thanks to these mechanisms of depression and persecution, the object of love stays as close to the ideal as possible. This is the state we consider normal. But when things around us change, when we ourselves change (in adolescence, for example), when we encounter other possibilities, other realities, when our relationships with our love objects deteriorate, then it becomes more and more difficult to preserve this ideal image through depression and persecution.

In every historical period that precedes an experience of falling in love, there is always a long preparation due to a slow change, a slow deterioration in relations with love objects. In this period, those two old mechanisms, depression and persecution, continue to function: we protect our ideal with all our strength, concealing the problem. The consequence is that the collective movement (falling in love) always strikes suddenly. "She was so kind and affectionate," says the abandoned husband, "she was so happy with me." In reality, she was already looking for an alternative, but she rejected it obsessively. She consciously forced herself to continue loving her husband; she made every effort to keep on considering him perfect, worthy of her love. In order to do so, however, she became at once more depressed and more uncommunicative. She had to direct more and more aggression against herself, constantly increasing the extent of her self-sacrifice. The ideal—the god—shows himself to be capable of surviving only if he is nourished by increasing sacrifices.

First—to continue the metaphor—he asked only for the first fruits, then the entire harvest, then the seed itself, and finally self-destruction. This is the *excessive depression* that precedes all collective movements as well as falling in love. In the face of self-destruction, even fear is mitigated, and other things, once experienced as seductions to be avoided, are now seen in a different light. Is there not perhaps life in them too? Is their difference as wicked as people say? The process continues to a *threshold* beyond which eros overflows the structures and floods prohibited territories; the violence that was self-directed for too long also overflows, uncontainable, overwhelming the rules that had kept it prisoner and destroying them: this is the *nascent state*. Now two forces are freed: one—eros— violently embraces with its force new objects which it instantly transforms into ideals; the other—violence— breaks with endured and accepted restraints. The experience is one of liberation, fullness of life, happiness. The possible opens before us and the pure object of eros appears, the unambivalent object, in which duty and pleasure coincide, in which all alienation is extinguished.

4

FALLING IN LOVE IS A DIVIDING OF WHAT WAS UNITED and a uniting of what was divided. This uniting, however, is quite specific because it appears as a structural alternative to an already structured relationship. The new structure radically challenges the old one and degrades it to something that has no value. In its place the new structure creates a new community based on an absolute value, an absolute right, and reorganizes everything around this right. This reorganization does not happen in an instant; it is a process. What does happen instantly is the appearance of *the pure object of eros.* It appears to us as a revelation. But the experience of falling in love is not this instant of revelation: it is a process in which the pure object of eros, having appeared in an instant, disappears, then reappears, disappears again and reappears richer, more concrete, impressing itself on us. When we fall in love, for a long time we keep on telling ourselves that we aren't in love. When the moment in which the extraordinary event was revealed to us has passed, we return to our everyday lives and think that it was something ephemeral. Much to our amazement, however, it comes to mind again and creates a desire, a torment, which subsides only when we hear the beloved's voice or see her (or him) once

more. But then it disappears again, and we tell ourselves
that it was an infatuation, that it doesn't matter at all. And
this may in fact be true, because in the beginning we cannot distinguish whether we have actually fallen in love,
whether we have experienced a radical restructuring of
the social world in which we are inserted and which is an
organic part of us. But if that desire continues to reappear
and *impresses itself on us*, then we are in love. Falling in
love is a process in which the other person, the one whom
we have encountered and who has responded to us, is impressed on us as an object full of desire. And this fact
compels us to reorganize everything, to rethink everything, beginning with our past. In reality, it is not a re-
thinking, but a remaking. It is actually a *rebirth*. The nascent state (of falling in love or of collective movements)
has this extraordinary capacity to remake the past.

In our everyday lives, we cannot remake the past. Our
past exists with its disappointments, its regrets, its bitterness. When we return to the past in our memory, we try
to heal some of the wounds that have remained open.
Why wasn't what I needed given to me? Why so much
effort, so much suffering, and then so little recognition?
Why didn't the person I love so much love me in return?
And why did I have to react with bitterness and hate to
remove her (or him) from my mind? Our past weighs on
our conscience. We protect ourselves from the past with
forgetfulness, with distractions, with the displacement
that renders it unconscious. But as Freud said, the unconscious is immortal. Nietzsche attributes human unhappiness to the spirit of revenge, and revenge is hatred of our

own past, of what cannot be changed. The will "is sullenly wrathful that time does not run back," says Zarathustra. " 'That which was'—that is what the stone which it cannot roll away is called." But Zarathustra promises, through the superman, precisely this liberation: "To redeem the past and to transform every 'It was' into an 'I wanted it thus!'—that alone do I call redemption!"*

What Nietzsche promises with the superman is exactly what happens in the nascent state: a historicization. The person in love (and often both lovers together) goes back over his past and realizes that what happened happened the way it did because at that time he made certain choices, and wanted to make them, but now he no longer does. The past is not hidden or denied; it is simply deprived of value. "Of course, I loved my husband, and I hated him too, but I don't hate him any more; I was wrong, but I can change." The past appears as *prehistory*, and true history now begins. So resentment, rancor and desire for revenge stop; what has no value, what does not count, can't be hated. This experience often provokes anguish and anxiety in the lovers. The woman I love talks about her past in front of me; she discusses her affairs, the man she was married to or lived with. At first she talks about him with bitterness, in a rage, and then gradually almost with tenderness. "He was mean to me," she says, "but he loves me and I care for him; I don't want to make him suffer; I'd like him to be happy." These words indi-

* Friedrich Nietzsche, *Thus Spoke Zarathustra*, trans. R. J. Hollingdale (Baltimore: Penguin Books, 1961), p. 161.

cate a detachment achieved because there is no longer any tension, fear, desire for revenge. But the same words can also be interpreted as a continuing love, and sometimes they arouse jealousy. The person who has fallen in love can often continue living with her husband (or his wife) without bitterness and with affection—as long as this does not pose any problems. Her past has acquired a new significance in the light of her new love. In the end, she can continue to love her own husband precisely because she is in love. The joy of this love makes him seem kind, sweet, good. It is generally the other person who does not accept this situation, who does not believe it, who wants the beloved all to himself. And since each of the lovers wants this exclusivity and this certainty, they are often forced to discard more than each of them would like.

The joy of a new love also generates another illusion. It leads the lover to believe that the people he leaves behind can accept his new love serenely, peacefully. He does not feel any hatred now, and he is not suffering any longer. "Let's be friends," he says, and he is sincere. He would even like to tell them of his new love, since the past is that distant and he bears no grudges. The *new community* in which he is participating can accept old things, old friendships and old relationships by transforming them. There are people who, before they fall in love, can no longer endure their own parents or their own children. Once they are in love, however, they discover a profound tenderness for their relations; their happy love leads them to rediscover it. And since they are not resentful any longer, since they no longer set store by the past, they believe that others will do the same. But this never happens. Even if the relationship has deteriorated, even if it has grown embittered and consists almost entirely of hatred, the effect of one person's falling in love is to provoke a terrible desire in the abandoned one, as if it made her love the man who at this point does not need her any longer and does not suffer any more because of her. What had become uninteresting in the ordinariness of everyday life becomes something essential again. This is comprehensible only if we keep in mind that it occurs in institutions, in social structures, and is frustrated by them. The abandoned person's loss devalues everything she is—her values, her self-image, her self-esteem. The one who has fallen in love does not realize the terrible offense he gives to the person he leaves behind, and this person cannot forgive him. So where the lover expected to find understanding, he finds denial, desperation, an argument. His love had brought into being a universal good, in which life is a joyous force, in which colors are alive, things beautiful. Eros that has found its object drives the negative, nonbeing, into the background, like a shadow. What was revealed to Parmenides at the beginning of Greek philosophy is an elementary experience of the nascent state: *being is and nonbeing is not.* But for the external world, for the social structure upset by this movement, all this is loss, a deprivation of being, and the world subsequently reacts (this is the *reaction* that always accompanies such movements) by saying "no," by opposing it. The disappointed father shouts or withdraws into silence. The husband who was constantly unfaithful discovers the value of fidelity. The wife who has grown unattractive and frowzy tries desperately to win back her husband by making herself beautiful, by discovering new interests. Even people who have built their conjugal relationship on sexual tolerance become rigid when confronted with their spouse's new love and experience it as a mortal offense. As a consequence, they hinder it by withholding their consent and creating insoluble problems. The husband who can no longer do anything to stop the new love says: "All right, leave, but you can't take the children; they stay with me." The wife says: "All right, go with her, but don't think I agree with this; you'll find me dead first." In this way, everything that was full of joy—those people, that husband or wife, those children who received value precisely from this nascent love—denies the radiant image of a world that says "yes," because they say "no" and demand a choice: him or the children, her or my death.

But love does not come into being to lose children, to kill someone, or to make anyone suffer. Love is the establishment of a new community, a happy shared life in which, in the absolute ingenuousness of its plan, everyone should recognize himself. The reaction denies this hope of harmony and demands a choice: either this or that. The history of falling in love is the history of the refusal to choose and of learning how to choose. In the nascent state, however, the demand to choose has the character of a dilemma. It is like asking a mother whose two children have been kidnapped to choose which of them must be killed. There is no solution.

The nascent state, both with collective movements and

with falling in love, always encounters a *dilemma*. Here too, as we have already said about transgression, it does not matter what dilemma arises. I have given two examples among many other possibilities, but there is no case in which a dilemma does not present itself. When fairy tales end with "and they lived happily ever after," the concluding silence does not designate merely the return of the everyday, the end of tension and hence of pathos. That silence also suppresses the appearance of a dilemma. In contrast, art, unlike fairy tales, presents the dilemma through the fiction of an insuperable obstacle that renders love impossible. The obstacle that is constantly thrown in the path of love signifies the dilemma. Tristram is divided between his affection for the king and his love for Iseult; Iseult between her affection for the king and her love for Tristram. Both Romeo and Juliet want to crush the inexorable laws of kinship and hatred, but they do not hate their parents. Love tends to separate the law from the person; it wants to establish other laws, other norms. It does not want to deny people; it wants to love them. But the laws speak through people; people incarnate the ancient laws and oppose the new justice. The law cannot be violated without confronting the people who incarnate it; this is the dilemma. And the law therefore always appears and requires falling in love to lose its *innocence*. Those who want to liberate sexuality, desire or eroticism by repudiating the existence of the dilemma, as if it were a product of history—the consequence of ignorance or class domination or a repressive education or some other thing—create a dreadful mystification. They produce a consoling ideology. It is like the person who eulogizes the revolution and then imagines it as a great celebration of friendship and love. This is the honeymoon of the revolution, the revolutionary nascent state. But then the revolutionary movement encounters internal and external obstacles, and it must choose. And here it can only be hoped that the revolution does not produce a slaughter, a bloodbath and terrible atrocities, that it does not repeat the barbarities of Hitler, Stalin and Pol Pot. Ignoring the fact that enthusiastic innocence will confront a dilemma means falling headlong into irrationality and violence. Yet the way the dilemma is confronted and resolved (or better yet, sidestepped) is the true history of falling in love and of the process by which it becomes a plan and an institution.

5

THE NASCENT STATE IS THE REVELATION OF AN AFFIR-
mative state of being. There is no motive at all for saying
"yes" to another person, no guarantee, but we say it any-
way. Anyone who falls in love has made a great many previous attempts, has tried to open himself to it many, many
times, but was not ready or did not meet a response. Yet
even when he meets a response, he may not know if it is a
true, total one. He is not sure of his own feelings, much
less those of another person. When someone falls in love,
he opens himself to a different existence without any
guarantee that it can be realized. It is a lofty song that is
never certain of finding an answer. Its greatness is desperately human, for it offers moments of happiness and eternity, creates a consuming desire for them, but cannot
provide any certainties. And when a response comes from
the other person, from the beloved, it appears as something undeserved, as a marvelous gift that the lover never
thought he could have. This gift comes wholly from the
other, from the beloved, by her own choice. Theologians
have a term to indicate this gift: they call it *grace*. And
when the beloved says that she loves him in return and
makes love to him, when the lover feels the other's total
abandon, then he is happy and time ceases to exist: that

moment becomes eternal for him. He will never forget it, never be able to. If the lover feels he is loved in return, he has only to remember this to bear any pain or difficulty. He will find refuge in being loved; it will be the source of every desire. But if one day the beloved leaves him, then that memory, precisely because it remains immortal, will be the reason for his unhappiness, and everything else will seem like nothing in comparison to what he has lost. And that memory will endure until another nascent state remakes the past.

We are aware of this terrible risk, but when we fall in love, we face it. We face it after opposing it with all our might, after we have rejected it many times. Falling in love, as we have said, is a revelation, a domination. We say "no" because we know what it means to say "yes," and we have no guarantee that the road to a new life is not the road to desperation. We say "no," we say that it was only an illusion, but then our mind becomes clear as a mirror, and on the one hand there is the gift, while on the other there is the nothingness of everyday life. And our mind discovers that it cannot choose what has no value, what is not good. The mind discovers that it can want only what is good, and that its everyday life is worth nothing next to what presents itself as good, next to what has value in itself. Our desire for this absolute good ensures that our every fear of the future will disappear. Every meeting with the beloved could be the final one. All that we desire is to be with her, since it may be for the last time. The dimension of the love that finds its object is *the present*, that instant which is worth as much as the lover's entire past and everything in the world. As a result, the happiness we feel in love always contains a note of sadness, because when we "make time stop," we know that in doing so we sacrifice every certainty and every resource. "Stopping time" means happiness, but it also means giving up strength and control over things. It is a renunciation of every power and every pride.

This plunge into a life with no certainty of the future, this stopping of time, is represented in art as death. Only the love that ends in death can serve as a device for expressing every uncertainty, every doubt, every desire of the person in love as well as their dissolution beyond past and future in that eternal present which cancels out every question. Hence death is the artistic signifier of the end of time which the lover experiences. It is a fascinating fiction that has the power to evoke in us every pain of the search for love, and this makes us relive the tormenting desire for the absent beloved to such an extent that there is no longer any desire, only the peace of being absorbed in her. When Werther dies, he "stops time" for himself and for Lotte. In reality, love as an existential fact is made up of moments of eternity which it continually transcends. When love is mutual, the other person says "yes" and later returns to say "yes" again. Time does not end; desire reproduces itself and encounters its object anew. Falling in love is a discovery, a loss and a rediscovery.

Of course, nothing guarantees the continuity of the mutual relationship, but there is always the experience of "grace" that maintains this trust. For falling in love is also trust, trusting oneself and trustingly abandoning oneself to the other person. Lovers are not jealous. There are certainly a great many individual differences in this sphere of experience, but falling in love tends to produce trust. The object of love appears as an unambivalent and hence good object. Falling in love is an experience of authenticity, of transparency, of truth. Lovers spend hours on end telling each other in detail about their lives because each wants to make the other participate in the totality of his being, which includes the past. And the other person listens to this past, fascinated, and sometimes envies those people who met her absolute good before she did, because she seems to have lost a precious opportunity for happiness. But she isn't worried. The rule that the past does not count, although incomprehensible in everyday life, is valid in the nascent state, as in the parable of the worker who was hired at the end of the day but accepts the same salary as those who began work in the morning.

Falling in love tends to result in a *fusion*, but it is a fusion of two different people. For love to occur, there must be a difference, and falling in love is a will, a drive to overcome this difference, which nonetheless exists and must exist. The beloved is interesting because she (or he) is different, because she bears her own unmistakable specificity. This specificity, this *uniqueness*, actually increases when we fall in love. We want to be loved insofar as we are unique, extraordinary, irreplaceable, absolutely ourselves. This cannot be achieved in organizations where all of us are replaceable, interchangeable. Nor can it be achieved in the everyday life of the family, because here we are unique and irreplaceable, but not extraordinary; and if we are unique, we are not exclusively so as an end in ourselves. Yet we desire to feel that we are this ultimate end. It is not enough, however, to be adored by someone who has no value, by someone who is replaceable. We want to be experienced as unique, extraordinary and indispensable by someone who is also unique, extraordinary and indispensable. For this reason, the experience of falling in love can only be monogamous: it is a claim of exclusivity and a recognition of the extraordinary made by someone who is so; it is an abandonment of ourselves to that man or woman who is the only person capable of giving pleasure, joy, life. Thus I am absolutely unique and she is absolutely unique; neither of us is interchangeable with any other person or thing. Every detail of her voice, her body, her gestures comes to signify this uniqueness. These details are found in her and in her alone, not in any other person in the world. She is extraordinarily unique and extraordinarily different, and what the lover finds amazing is that he is recognized by a creature so unique, so totally herself, so unlike any other person. Each of us is different from every other person, as we know, but it is only when we fall in love that our irreducible individuality is grasped and appreciated completely. A sure and unmistakable sign of love is this appreciation of the other person's specificity and uniqueness. The appreciation we feel coming from her allows us to appreciate ourselves, to give nourishing value to our ego. This is the movement of individuation. But at the same time the experience of falling in love initiates a second movement, that of fusion, which is in a certain sense opposed to the first one. Fusion is directed toward producing a union of wills. A mutual love means that both lovers want what is important for each of them. Individuation differentiates,

gives value to differences, makes them into absolute
values, insures that my beloved's preferences are both law
and the ideal for me, and that my preferences acquire an
exemplary value in my eyes. Fusion occurs so that these
different preferences merge to make up a single will. But
precisely because these differences and these preferences
have become important, they tend to prevail and clash.
Love is also a struggle. When we are in love, each of us
tries to show off our best part, what we feel is most ours,
most true, and we desire this to be appreciated. But the
other person appreciates something else more and reveals
it to us. So since love leads us to adopt the beloved's point
of view, we must remake our self-image. The very desire
to please the beloved leads us to change ourselves. In this
way, each of us imposes his (or her) point of view on the
other person and changes himself to give the other person pleasure. In all of this there is no imposition, but
a continual deciphering, a continual discovery. Every
aspect of the other person's behavior—every gesture,
every glance—becomes a symbol to interpret. And we in
turn are continual producers of symbols. The nascent
state is a proliferation of signs. In this process, which en-
compasses the present and the past, nature too is involved.
Rain and sunshine, the shape of a cloud grow rich with
values, come to signify something that is connected with
the beloved and with our love for her; they have a meaning,
indicate a direction. Since there is an obstacle, since the
other person is different, since her response is never absolutely certain or at least never perfectly suited to the
question, the most casual incidents, things, combinations
become signals for interpretation, invitations, denials,

omens. Every place where something significant happened becomes sacred.

Love produces a sacred geography of the world. That place, that house, that particular view of the sea or the mountains, that tree become sacred symbols of the beloved or of love. They become sacred zones, temples, because they hosted one of love's eternal moments or an omen. And as space is sanctified, so is time. If the period of happiness in the nascent state is the eternal present, the conjunction of these moments of eternity constitutes a liturgical year with its holy days. They are points of meaning and value, memories of exemplariness, of pain, of happiness, or even merely moments that are significant for the other person and become sacred for us. In this way, the experience of falling in love, as it unfolds, produces an objective sanctity. Space is composed of fixed points, while time is discontinuous, composed of significant days, and both are sacred, as in religions. Falling in love reestablishes the division between the sacred and the profane and has a very strong sense of sacrilege. Even at a distance of years or decades, lovers who are now separated will not be able to get through certain days without being upset, will not be able to return to certain places without being flooded by nostalgia. This sacred space and time are immortal because they define the circumstances under which the eternal present, the stopping of time, is made objective. Forgotten, they survive in the unconscious. Only another nascent state can erase them to create a new space and a new time.

6

EVERYDAY LIFE IS CHARACTERIZED BY DISAPPOINTMENT. We always have so many things to do. Some of them may be a pleasure for us, but the great majority by far are requests from other people. What others ask of us is always urgent, always merits priority, and if we don't do it at once, they will reproach us, hold a grudge against us, punish us. The order of things does not have us at its center; we are not its principal agent. This is the result of the pressures put on us. We never achieve what we really desire, and at a certain point, we wind up not even knowing if we want it. In everyday life, our desire appears to us in the guise of fantasies: "How beautiful it would be if . . ." But something always happens to frustrate us. Our friends, male and female alike, always have something else to do, or have no desire to do what we would like, or want to when we don't and ask us at the most inopportune moment. If we say, "No, let's do it another time," our friend takes offense, and we lose interest just as he or she does. All this is disappointment: we have the feeling that something is desirable, but it always eludes us because we must always do something else. In everyday life, we wind up being absorbed by this continual necessity to do something else for some other person; our life is reduced to doing something else. Never do we feel that we are really understood; never do we experience a profound satisfaction; never do our desires completely coincide with those of other people. This is a state that always seems to be on the verge of ending; in fact, it seems impossible that things can go on like this, in such a stupid, bitter way. And yet it continues for months, for years—dark years of waiting for something completely unknown, years of continual disappointment, years without history and without true happiness, in which we "keep on going."

The profound attraction that falling in love excites in each of us is due to the fact that it introduces into this darkness a blinding light and an absolute danger. Falling in love frees our desire, puts it at the center of everything. We desire, we want something absolutely for ourselves. Everything we do for the beloved isn't a question of doing something else for another person; we do it for ourselves, to be happy. Our entire life is aimed toward a goal whose reward is happiness. Our desires coincide with those of the beloved. Falling in love transports us to a higher life where either everything is won or everything is lost. Everyday life is characterized by the necessity of always doing something else, of choosing between things that interest others: it is a choice between greater or less disappointment. When we fall in love, however, the choice is between everything and nothing. It is as if each day we win what is unthinkable in everyday life: a kingdom, power, happiness, glory. But this kingdom can always be lost—and in a single battle. The polarity of everyday life is between tranquillity and disappointment; that of love is between ecstasy and torment. Everyday life is an eternal purgatory. When we fall in love, there is only heaven or hell; either we are saved or we are damned.

I realize that this idea raises two contrasting kinds of objections. The first is this: of course, these misunderstandings and continual frustrations happen in everyday life, but the reason is that social relationships have not been constructed correctly. If a married couple feel that they are doing something that doesn't satisfy them, if they think that they really don't understand each other, they need a marriage counselor or something similar. With therapy (psychoanalytic, behavioral, Gestalt, Lacanian, Reichian, Catholic, Buddhist or Marxist), these misunderstandings and conflicts will disappear. Behind this therapeutic attitude lies a concept of ideal normality that is entirely based on fantasy. I don't deny the value of individual, social or political therapies; they serve to create a situation in which suffering is reduced, social conditions are improved, and society advances. But they can't change at all the existential structure of everyday life. A husband and wife who undergo psychoanalysis will get along better and hurt each other less, but they will not experience a continually full life.

The second objection is aimed at the description of love as a tension between ecstasy and torment. True love, it is said, is a state of constant happiness, constant understanding, perfect agreement, in which minor disagreements are settled naturally. Otherwise there is no true love. True love, someone else adds, is achieved gradually, with patience and wisdom. This is Fromm's view, for example, and he offers everyone his prescription for happiness, "the art of loving." In reality, behind these assertions lies nothing else but the fairy tale myth, "and they lived happily ever after," the illusion of a daily or, in fact, a perpetual serenity and joy, which no one has ever experienced.

I said that there were two objections, but there is actually only one. Marriage counselors and therapists are concerned only with that fairy tale myth of a life lived "happily ever after," which they promise left and right as if it were the easiest thing to achieve. All the psychologists, sociologists, social engineers and the various kinds of therapists basically promise the same thing: complete and continuous happiness. In doing so, they are like those quacks who used to travel around with a little bottle containing the elixir of long life or eternal youth. But if eternal youth is biologically impossible, if it is biological nonsense, the same must be said of the continuous happiness and tranquillity expressed in the formula "and they lived happily ever after." This is nonsense on the level of existential experience.

So what we are dealing with is a myth, a very widespread myth that all of us constantly reinforce without even realizing it. At this point, we should ask ourselves: what is the origin of this myth? We have described everyday life as tranquillity and disappointment, love as ecstasy and torment. Each of these two dialectic pairs has a positive and a negative pole. The myth arises when we take only the positive poles and join them (contentment and happiness) without the negative ones (disappointment and torment). We can also see how it is possible for the myth to arise. The desire for happiness, the happiness savored in the nascent state of falling in love, is always alive in us as nostalgia. Trapped in everyday life, in the world of disappointment, we desire a fuller, more exalting life, something that is true and authentic; we desire the happiness of the nascent state and its ecstasy. We also recall that there was torment in this state, but we want to forget about it, and we imagine that we can rediscover the eternity of love in its greatest splendor and purity.

Yet when we fall in love, when everything in us is passion and happiness, but also torment, anxiety and desire, we want to prolong the happy state, we desire it to endure, to become serenity, tranquillity, not entangled with everything that always accompanies it. There are people who can't bear the tension of falling in love; they would like to restrain it immediately, to make it ordinary, domestic, controllable. This is how the desire for peace, tranquillity and serenity springs from the experience of falling in love.

The truth is that whoever is immersed in everyday life cannot reach that spasmodic intensity of desire and will which produces happiness. To do so, it is necessary to break with everyday life, to cross the prohibited river of transgression. And this isn't something we can decide whenever we like. The experience of falling in love "appears" when its structural conditions have slowly matured; it is an "event" that impresses itself on us. In the same way, when we fall in love, we cannot reach and maintain the state of serene tranquillity. Our love is not in our grasp; it transcends us, pulls us and forces us to change. To succeed in transforming this thing into the serenity of everyday life, we must destroy it. And many people, I repeat, men as well as women, have no peace until they have transformed the splendid experience of their love into something controllable, circumscribed, defined. The price, however, is that they stop falling in love and the ecstasy disappears. What remains is everyday banality, a tranquil serenity constantly interrupted by boredom, bitterness or disappointment.

In the everyday, then, there is a desire for the extraordinary; in the extraordinary, a desire for the everyday. In the everyday, there is a desire for ecstasy; in the extraordinary, a desire for tranquillity. These two desires, neither of which can be realized, are joined together to make up that "happily ever after" life which, in our time, has replaced the mythical elixir of eternal youth and the philosopher's stone.

7

IS IT POSSIBLE TO LOVE TWO PEOPLE AT THE SAME TIME? Of course. Is it possible to love one person and fall in love with another? Of course. Is it possible to fall in love with two people? No. Each of us loves many people: our mother and father, our friends, our children. None of these relationships excludes the others or takes anything away from them. In the same way, a man can love two wives and a woman two husbands. Each of them can fall in love with another person while continuing to love the first. In fact, we can say that this is the rule. But it is impossible to fall in love with two different people. At first glance this limitation seems absurd. We constantly hear people say, "I've fallen in love with both of them," or, "I don't know who I love more." These expressions occur in two different situations. The first we can call the preparation for falling in love. As we have already said, a person who is about to fall in love looks for someone who responds to him in a certain way, and he often feels that he has found her. In other words, he often starts to fall in love. And since he may happen to meet many people, he starts to fall in love many times, occasionally superimposing one person on another. This is why he can say, "I'm in love with both of them." This becomes easier to say when two different women fall in love with him at the same time. Since he is ready for love and finds a positive response in both of them, a group of three individuals is created. Now let us suppose that the two women who love him are close friends or sisters. Together they form a closed group of which he is the center. Situations of this kind are anything but rare. In collective movements we often find groups of women who adore the same leader. Didn't Freud say that the crowd is formed by individuals who identify with each other and at the same time with the leader? By means of an apparently uninterrupted transition, then, we have passed from the collective movement of two individuals in love to the collective movement of the group. In reality, however, the transition is not so smooth. Let us consider a group whose center is a leader adored by his women. Can we say that he has fallen in love with any of them? No. Each of them, like each of his followers, is replaceable. In a collective movement involving a group, no one is indispensable; everyone is interchangeable. This also applies to the group made up of three individuals. Even with three people, the collective continues to exist if one leaves. Only in the case of the couple does the collective disappear when one member leaves. Only in the couple is the individual indispensable in his absolute specificity and uniqueness; he cannot be replaced by any other person. Only in the couple is the individual the objective condition for the existence of the collective. The collective is realized through the individual and cannot do without him. Thus the collective movement involving two persons, the experience of falling in love, has something specific about it, something absolutely different from other movements. Expressions like "I'm in love with both of them" therefore indicate a state of indeterminacy or transition which can lead to a collective structure or to love or to nothing at all. The love of a leader is sometimes a detached idealization, but it can also be a one-sided affection. Many individuals, in fact, can truly fall in love with the same person without that person being truly in love with any of them. A relationship of this kind, a one-sided love, surrounds charismatic leaders or a celebrated actress or simply a fascinating woman.

Now let us return to the problem where we began. We have said that we can love many people at the same time and fall in love with another, different person. In such a case, the new love is the point of departure for a restructuring of our affections. The people we love become components of ourselves, of our total reality, of that individuality we want recognized and loved when we fall in love. In other words, the experience of falling in love always happens between two individuals who each have a personal history, a system of affections, of preferences. Falling in love, insofar as it is the overcoming of a barrier, always means a restructuring of this system of affections. Something that was essential before is abandoned, considered devoid of value, while something else is retained and must be integrated into the new love. For example, if two individuals who are married and have children fall in love, each of them separates his spouse from his children in his system of affections. Each can and wants to do without his spouse; in this respect, each wants to change his behavior

completely. This is not so where the children are concerned. The children can be integrated into the new love.
The spouse ceases to be a part of the nucleus that makes
up the self asking to be recognized; the children, however,
are part of it. Yet the encounter is between two isolated
people. No children are involved in it. The encounter involves two isolated individuals. The question and answer
occur before the children appear. The individual seeks
love for himself, not for his children. The process of falling in love, then, consists precisely in *integrating into the
relationship those parts of the self that had at first been
excluded,* and hence the children as well. But the one who
has fallen in love is in love with the other person, not with
his children. The children are loved inasmuch as they are
loved by the other person, not for themselves. And they
may even be an obstacle, sometimes an insuperable one, to
the unfolding of love. They may oppose it, for example, or
they may become an instrument of pressure and black-
mail used by the two families, thereby creating a dilemma. In every case, falling in love is always a meeting of
two isolated individuals, each of whom carries in and with
himself a system of relationships, wanting to retain some
and restructure others. To represent falling in love as a
meeting between two isolated individuals who seek absolute solitude and have no impediments, no bonds, is a falsification. In reality, they seek an absolute meeting of
their individual natures, but at the same time an integra-
tion of the immediate circumstances in which they are
involved. Not one or the other, but both of these
things.

The desire for complete, constant, definitive isolation is an expression of a problem, an attempt to avoid the burden that the lover's situation puts on the new love. When the weight of the lover's surrounding reality becomes unbearable, when it becomes impossible to integrate that part of the self composed of his preexisting affections, his new love tends to withdraw from the world, to become a liberated and liberating area in which to find refuge and peace and from which to depart anew to confront the world. If the two lovers find themselves in the same situation, then what prevails is the desire to escape, to avoid the pressures of that situation completely, to give their life together a firm footing so that they may later regain what they had lost. If, however, the problem exists for only one lover, he will be the one to conceive of his new love as a refuge, as a liberated and liberating area in which to avoid the pressures of his situation. Yet this project eventually conflicts with the other person's desire to realize her own love in the world, in a concrete way, integrating what can be integrated and discarding what must be discarded. For one lover, love becomes a moment of pure escape, a vacation from the world, the haven, a happy isle on which to land and take refuge, the rose garden in the middle of the desert of existence. For the other, this fantasy is an evasion because she wants to transform the world into a garden. This is an example of how the new love between two individuals produces two different plans for an extraordinary life. Here the plans are incompatible, and the lovers must abandon one of them or both, in which case their love is torn apart by contradictions and comes to an end.

I have said that it is possible to love one person and fall in love with another, but impossible to fall in love with two people at the same time. The experience of falling in love is in fact a process of restructuring every relationship around an individual. The new love creates the absolute direction in which the lover moves. Two experiences of falling in love are impossible because they mean moving with all the strength of our spirit toward two absolute but different objectives.

What happens, then, when two lovers have a child? Let us consider the case where one of the lovers does not desire it. As a result, when the child is born, the one who was against it experiences the other's love for the child as a true and proper betrayal, an abandonment. In Islamic-Persian law, Eblis (Satan) rebels against God because after He created man, He asked the archangel of light to love him. But Eblis answers that he cannot, because he loves God alone, and he cannot accept God's love for man. So he prefers to incur God's anger, to lose Him, rather than share Him with another creature. Now let us consider the case where both lovers want the child. The child is born desired and becomes a new pole around which love revolves. Yet even in this situation the experience of falling in love ends. It is difficult to admit this fact. There of course exists an ancient popular adage that says a child strengthens love and rescues a love that is in danger. But this refers to love, not to falling in love. The child in fact becomes an object of love for both lovers. Both fall in love with him at the same time. Their relationship now depends on the existence of a third person, no longer on themselves alone. The egotistic and absolute claims of their individual personalities give way not to the equally unique claims of another individual personality, but in favor of a third. Neither is essential to the other any more; neither is the other's god. Both lovers bow in adoration to a nascent god who is external to them. And if a difference or an inattention arises between them, each can find refuge in the child. This is especially true of the mother, who has carried the child in herself, who nourishes him, who is, at least for his first months of life, the child's absolute. In reality, the birth of a child is almost always a true and proper experience of falling in love for the mother. All her interests, all her cares, all her anxieties are focused on the child. This new exclusivity is incompatible with the old one. Before the Oedipus complex, what dominates the family scene is the Laius complex, the father's envy of the son or, better, of the mother-son couple, which as an absolute couple replaces the one originally formed by the two lovers. So the birth of the child—the love for the child —cements the union and stabilizes the love, but puts an end to the experience of falling in love. Paradoxically, this experience can continue if an external force separates the lovers, or if their love becomes one-sided and hence unhappy, as when one of them is jealous of the child.

The discontinuity represented by the birth of a child is hidden by our culture. And in general it is with surprise that each of us notices that the other overlooks us or no longer has that enthusiasm and total desire she had before. In reality, everything has changed. A potentially permanent structure has been substituted for an intrinsically unstable one like falling in love. Even if this experience ends, even if love disappears and the two people separate, the collective now survives in two couples, mother-and-child and father-and-child.

8

IN GENESIS WE READ THAT GOD "DROVE OUT THE MAN; and he placed at the east of the garden of Eden Cherubims, and a flaming sword which turned every way, to keep the way of the tree of life." In the nascent state man tears the flaming sword from the cherubim's hand and enters the Garden of Eden. But he is unable to stay there and make the Garden his home and land. The nascent state is by definition transitory. It is not a pause, but a motion, a motion toward; and to arrive is to leave this state. Falling in love, when all goes well, ends in love; the movement, when it succeeds, produces an institution. But the relationship between falling in love and love itself, between nascent state and institution, is comparable to that between taking off or flying and landing, between being in the sky above the clouds and firmly setting foot on the ground again. Consider another image, that of the flower and the fruit. The fruit issues from the flower, but they are two different things. When there is fruit, there is no longer any flower. And there is really no point in asking if the flower is better than the fruit or vice versa. By the same token, there is no point in asking whether the nascent state is better than the institution. One does not exist without the other. Life is made up of both. Still, there is no point in confusing them, because they are distinct. The way of feeling, thinking and living in the nascent state is different from that of everyday, institutional life. It isn't merely a question of different thoughts, but a difference in ways of thinking, *a different conceptual system.*

We can begin our discussion of this difference at any point. In everyday life, the aims we set for ourselves, the things we try to obtain, all take into account the means we have at our disposal. We don't set for ourselves goals that cannot be realized. Our desires, however, are limitless. If the genie in fairy tales appeared and asked us to name three things we want, we would be perplexed, and a bizarre list would come to mind. Would we like to be very rich? Or to be healthy? Do we want these things only for ourselves, or for our loved ones too? Do we want to be young forever, and will we reserve this wish for ourselves or include others as well? We could avoid this difficulty by asking for "happiness," but happiness isn't a thing; the problem is to identify the "things" that make us happy. A person who has fallen in love would know very well what to ask for: "I want her to love me in return." And if two more wishes remain, he would add: "I want to keep on loving her, and I want her to keep on loving me." This person has a very precise, limited desire. Yet in setting this goal for himself, he doesn't consider the means available to him. No one falls in love and says, "Since I have the means to make her love me, I am deciding to fall in love with her." First he falls in love, first he desires the other person's love, and then he searches for the means to win it, to make her love him. Another characteristic of everyday life is that it really does not involve a distinction between *essential needs* and *nonessential needs.* This distinction does exist in the nascent state. Everything that helps us reach the one we love and make her love us is essential. The rest is worthless. Eating well is very nice if it gives pleasure to the one we love, but in itself it doesn't matter at all to us. To meet her, to be with her, we are willing to make the most tiring journeys, to go without eating and sleeping, and the effort doesn't bother us; in fact, it makes us happy. We do everything we would find unbearable in our everyday lives without realizing it.

In everyday life the principle of calculable exchange applies. If I give you something, I want something in return, and it must have the same value as what I give you. In the nascent state, however, the rule of *communism* prevails: each person gives according to his abilities and receives according to his needs. No record is kept of what I give and what I receive. Each gives gifts to the other: things that seem beautiful to him, something that speaks of himself, that will remind her of him, but also things that please her, that she has mentioned or seen. The gift is often a sudden act, a spontaneous gesture that symbolizes the gift of the lover's self, his own total availability. But the lover does not demand a gift in return, does not expect to be reciprocated. When the gift is given, the account is immediately paid up: the other person has only to appreciate it and be satisfied. Her joy is worth more than any object. So between the two lovers there is gift-giving, but without any exchange. Each lover gives what he can and receives what he needs. When a lover starts counting gifts, when he says, "I have given you a gift, but you haven't given me one," the experience of falling in love is about to end. When each lover demands an account of the giving and receiving, it has completely ended.

Connected to communism is the experience of *equality*, an equality that has nothing to do with the absence of differences. In fact, each lover is totally desired insofar as he has a unique and unmistakable individuality. Here equality stands for the absolute equality of rights, the right of each lover to make demands. When we fall in love, there are no preestablished rights. There is rather an equality of power. Since the lover's fulfillment of his desire depends totally on the beloved, each of them has an immense power, even a total power, over the other. But unless we are confronted with a one-sided love, this power is symmetrical. Every lover is at the mercy of the person he loves.

Another dimension of the nascent state is that of *truth* and *authenticity*. Falling in love is a search for our deepest authenticity, an attempt to be fundamentally ourselves. This is achieved thanks to the other person, to a dialogue with her, to the meeting in which each of us looks to the other for recognition, acceptance, understanding, approval and redemption of what has been and what actually is. The remaking of the past, of which I have already spoken, makes it safe; each of us can speak of the past, and when we do, when we tell the beloved about our previous life, we free ourselves from it. But in order to free ourselves, in order to be "redeemed from the past," we must tell the truth; only "the truth shall make us free."

So each of us is redeemed, telling the whole truth to the other person, making ourselves totally transparent by telling her about ourselves. There is no similar experience in everyday life. We can tell the truth to a stranger, but telling it doesn't help us in the least because he doesn't have any power over us. Only by telling the truth to the person who is the source of value can we be redeemed from what we have been and change, that is, become what we must in order to achieve what is most valuable to us. In psychoanalysis the patient tells the truth because, thanks to the transference, the process that spontaneously occurs when we fall in love is partly reproduced. But the strength of the nascent state shatters, in a few hours or a few moments, the unconscious barriers that sometimes last for years in psychoanalysis. This is possible because the lovers no longer fear the past. They make a mutual confession, and each of them has the power to absolve the other of his past.

We should not be surprised if we continually find religious references in our inquiry. In reality, the profound dynamics of the nascent state had previously been expressed only in the language of metaphysics and religion. To a large extent, our task consists of bringing theology back to earth, of recasting in human terms what until now has been described in terms of a relationship with God. Confession and absolution are thus two essential components of the nascent state. Lovers continually interrogate each other about what they are thinking. "What are you thinking?" is a spontaneous question for the person who has fallen in love. Deep down he means: "Are you thinking of me?" But a "yes" isn't enough. He wants to know about the other, about her life, her most secret thoughts; he wants her to be totally transparent in all her richness and concreteness, so that he can insert himself there not only as an authentic object of love, but also as an interpreter, a consolation, a guide. In this sense, it isn't enough for the other person to answer, "I'm thinking of you"; she must always indicate the real, concrete, individual direction of her thoughts. The "of you" is always the point of departure and arrival, but the journey is through the richness of that concrete reality which is transfigured and transubstantiated by love. Here is another religious word: transubstantiation, alteration of substance. Once a thing that was banal or simply dreary is spoken of or related, once this detail is accepted and inserted into the discourse of love, it emerges transfigured, endowed with value. The same thing happens with a defect, a weakness, a pain, an illness. As I have said, the person who is in love loves even the other's wounds, all the internal organs of her body (her liver, her lungs) and her soul (her childhood, her feelings toward her mother and father, her love for a doll). And since falling in love is also a resistance to love, a separation, a desire to be separated, this not wanting the other person must also be spoken, confessed, overcome and absolved.

Let us take another step forward. Only the object of our love has value in itself. This distinction between what has value in itself and what does not is the basis of *metaphysical thought*. Thus we can say that the metaphysical way of thinking applies in the nascent state. This way of thinking leads us to draw an absolute distinction between what has value in itself, and hence is real, and what is incidental. It is a division that runs through everything, ourselves included. Insofar as we are in agreement with reality, we are transfigured; we are bearers of values and absolute rights. Insofar as we are not in agreement with reality, we have no value; we are nothing at all. But since falling in love is a process, there is a constant movement of things, objects and experiences from one level to another, a constant metaphysical transition from what is incidental to what is real, and from what is real back to what is incidental. On the one hand, then, there is transfiguration (or transubstantiation), while on the other, there is degradation. I have a pin, and I want to give it to the person I love. She accepts it; she's pleased. She takes it with her. It becomes part of her, a little piece of me in her. Now let us suppose that we've quarreled, and I am upset. Yet when I meet her, I see that she is wearing my pin. At this point, the pin undergoes a transformation: it becomes the beloved's mouth and body; it tells me, "I still love you." The person who says "yes" is incorporated into the object. But there may be something about me that does not please my beloved, a certain style of clothing, an accessory. She tells me about it, and instantly the value of that object is degraded. Even if the object is costly, it is no longer worth anything to me.

Let us now return to our point of departure. The many ways of thinking and feeling we have described (moment-eternity, happiness, absolute goals, self-limitation of needs, equality, communism, authenticity and truth, the real and the incidental, and so on) are permanent, structural properties of the nascent state. In this state, we think, feel and judge in a radically different way. The extraordinary experience is not something that happens to us, that occurs in the external world; we are the ones who have changed, and because of this we see a different sky and earth, a different kind of men and women, a different kind of nature. The nascent state is an attempt to remake the world, starting with this different way of thinking and living; it is an attempt to achieve in the world this experience of absolute solidarity and the end of all alienation and uselessness. It therefore begins with what is desirable in itself, what is not completely given in the world. It is the attempt to achieve in the world the greatest possible degree of that absolute solidarity we have experienced. So it is an exploration of the possible, starting from the impossible, an attainment of paradise on earth. This is why I said at the beginning of this chapter that in the nascent state man tears the flaming sword from the cherubim's hand and enters the Garden of Eden. Of course, he can't make it his permanent residence; the experience of falling in love doesn't last forever: the extraordinary always coexists with the ordinary and becomes ordinary again. But it is the Garden of Eden. We are all familiar with it, we have all been there, we have all lost it, and we all know how to recognize it.

9

DANTE WROTE THAT LOVE "SWIFTLY SEIZES THE GEN-tle heart" and "spares no one from loving." What does the first statement mean? We have seen that the person who falls in love is predisposed to do so, that this experience happens when there are certain preconditions, when a certain preparation has taken place, when there have already been attempts and rehearsals. The person who falls in love has already tried to do so or has done so many times. The propensity to fall in love is indicated by *gentilezza* ["gentility" or "gentleness"] in the language of the *dolce stil nuovo*. There is an element of truth in this, since the tension that leads to the nascent state can have many outlets. Some people become religious converts, others join a political group, and still others fall in love. The experience of falling in love is already in some way predetermined by culture and by a psychological disposition. The very phrase "falling in love" is a cultural product, the result of a process in which a certain kind of experience is defined and transformed in a particular way. In ancient Greece and Rome, people certainly experienced nascent states of love, but they did not speak of falling in love. In the Islamic world, we can find a very rich tradition of mystical love poetry, but there was no literature similar to what the Christian Middle Ages later defined as the "recognized image" of falling in love. The psychological disposition to seek a solution in the nascent state—Dante's *gentilezza*—can also be opposed and inhibited by other cultural currents, by other ideologies.

Dante's second statement, that love "spares no one from loving," contains both a truth and a misunderstanding. In fact, the attempt to fall in love almost always fails. Even when one person falls in love, very often he is not loved in return, or at least not with the same intensity or in the same way. Yet there is also an element of truth in Dante's remark: when two people who are really prepared for love meet each other, it is very likely that they will in fact fall in love, that they will "recognize" each other. The explanation for this phenomenon can be found in what we have said in the preceding chapter. The nascent state is a completely different way of thinking, seeing, feeling and living. People who find themselves in this situation, in this state, understand each other profoundly. Although their personal histories are very different, they share the exact same relationship to the world. This is why in great collective movements thousands and thousands of people who differ in age and social class "recognize" each other and form a collective unit, a "we." The same thing happens when two people fall in love. The nascent state instantly creates *recognition* or *understanding* on a profound, intuitive level. Ramón Lull, the famous medieval mystic, writes: "Lover and Beloved are distinct beings, which agree, without any contrary element or diversity in

Essence."* This "Essence" is the *distinctive structure of the nascent state.* From it derives that very special experience in which two lovers who are completely different nonetheless have a mysterious and very strong spiritual affinity. This spiritual affinity, however, did not exist before; it came into being when the lovers encountered each other. Before they met, they spoke two different languages; now they speak the same language. With the nascent state, the profound structure of their way of thinking—what transcends their individual personalities—has become the same. The fact that every experience of the nascent state has the same distinctive structure ensures that even two people who speak such different languages as French and German and know little of each other's language can fall in love and understand each other. In the religious tradition, this is indicated by the gift of tongues, the glossolalia.

But Dante's remark also says something else. The nascent state has the power to arouse its own properties in others. When one person falls in love with another, he always evokes in her an awakening, an emotion. The lover tends to draw the beloved into his love. If the other person is ready for love, an encounter may take place, and they may simply fall in love. But it may also happen that the other person already has someone who interests her, in which case the lover's amorous poetry does indeed awaken her love, but for another person. She is trans-

* Ramón Lull, *The Book of the Lover and the Beloved*, trans. E. Allison Peers (New York: The Paulist Press, 1978), p. 66.

ported to a higher level of feeling, but the person who is the object of these sentiments is not the one who evoked them.

These different possibilities lead us to ask a crucial question: when two individuals fall in love, do they love each other equally, or does one person love more than the other? Falling in love is an individual, internal transformation in search of its object. At the start of every experience of falling in love, only one person is enamored. Most of these initial attempts end almost immediately. In some cases, however, the process continues, and we can have two outcomes. The lover may have made the right choice, and the other person may also be disposed to fall in love. So a nascent state involving two people develops, and the experience of falling in love is mutual. Yet there are also a great many instances in which the other person has only a desire for love or for adventure, or is attracted erotically or intellectually by the lover. As a result, she does not fall in love. This does not mean that she refuses his love; in fact, she may be flattered by it. But she does not undergo any internal change, doesn't enter into the nascent state, and participates only in the lover's experience of this state. She herself may think that she has fallen in love. But this is merely a reflex action because she accepts and participates in the symbols of the other person, who speaks the language of love. Seeing these two together, only an attentive eye would notice that one has fallen deeply in love, the other much less so. This kind of unequal relationship occurs very frequently and can last a long time; it can even lead to marriage. A deep affection is gradually established between the two lovers. But if this relationship confronts any serious obstacles, if one of the lovers is already married, for example, or has children or must be away for a long time, the difference becomes apparent. In the end, the person who has been "drawn" into falling in love can do without the other, while the one who is truly in love cannot. The former knows she has alternatives; the latter knows he does not. Thus the person who is drawn into love calmly states her conditions: "I'm here, and I love you. Solve your problems and come back. But don't show up until you solve them." She feels these problems are the other person's, not hers as well; in a word, she says to him: "Get yourself together." When both people fall in love, however, each of them tends to invade the other's territory, to think that every problem is "ours," and that only "we" can solve it.

Now let us consider another case of unequal love. All men and women are not the same; there are profound differences of sensibility, intelligence, culture and creativity among them. When a creative person falls in love, he becomes more and more creative and increases his capacity to enrich life with the fruits of his imagination. So he constructs fantastic labyrinths or enchanted cities and inhabits them as if they were real. Artists, poets and scientists live in the imaginary universe they have created, and when they fall in love, they tend to transport the person they love to this world of theirs. Its fascination is great, but often the disappointment it provokes is also great. Most people want concrete achievements, and so when they are faced with these fantastic creations, they have the feeling that something is unreal or simply false. There are differences that falling in love cannot erase: the complex person can understand the simple one, but the simple person cannot understand the complex one; to the simple person, complexity seems like falsehood or madness. Dostoevsky could understand the girl he had fallen in love with during his trip to Italy, but she could not understand him at all. When we read Goethe's *The Sorrows of Young Werther*, we can see the gulf that exists between Werther-Goethe and the simple Lotte. In Virginia Woolf, we constantly feel the loneliness of the genius who cannot be understood.

Let us keep in mind that when the simple person falls in love, he undergoes a transformation that puts him near the poets. The language of the nascent state is, as we have seen, the language of mysticism, theology and poetry. If the love between two people is unequal, the one who is truly in love tends to create an imaginary, poetic universe. The one who is less so has precise, concrete requests. But the nascent state is, in itself, an exploration of the possible, starting from the impossible; there is no pedantic assurance about what should and can be done. This is why the person who is less in love reproaches the lover for living in an unreal world where everything is play or fantasy and where there is a superabundant creation of symbols, metaphors or gifts; the person who is less in love, because of his aridity, senses the artifice in these things. When there is an unequal love, the person who loves less always reproaches the lover for not being very sensitive, for being an egotist, for living in daydreams or for being obscure.

Yet it is always the person who is deeply in love who incessantly poses, in a thousand different ways, the essential question: "Do you love me?" And she is the one who gives the gifts.

10

WE HAVE SAID THAT THE PERSON WHO FALLS IN LOVE IS the one who is predisposed to do so, who is available. Does this mean, then, that we fall in love when we feel the desire to fall in love? Does this mean that the person who feels the strong, consuming desire for a powerful new love is predisposed to fall in love? No. There is no relation at all between the desire for love and truly falling in love. There are people who feel this desire for many years, who in their meetings with others search for that unique person whom they can love and who can love them in return. But they never encounter this person. They blame their failure on bad luck, on where they go, on the fact that they're hard to please. Very often they feel that they have met the person; they experience an emotion, a desire, a longing to see her (or him) again. But it's like a flash of lightning and vanishes. Almost always they get the feeling that they have met someone who isn't really interested in them. They sense an aridity and an indifference around themselves. They passionately desire to be loved, they expect to meet the person who will answer "yes," but no one responds. They feel that they are seeking desperately. But are they really seeking? There's reason to wonder, because if by chance someone should respond, then they realize that something about her isn't right. It may be a physical characteristic, or the fact that she's too old or too young, too naïve or too sophisticated, too enthusiastic or too cool. In reality, people like this are not predisposed to fall in love, even if they desire it. The sort of love they long for so much is not a need to break completely with the past, a need to examine their life and to expose themselves to the risk of something totally new.

No one can fall in love if he is even partially satisfied with what he has or who he is. The experience of falling in love originates in an extreme depression, an inability to find something that has value in everyday life. The "symptom" of the predisposition to fall in love is not the conscious desire to do so, the intense desire to enrich our lives; it is the profound sense of being worthless and of having nothing that is valuable and the shame of not having it. This is the first sign that we are prepared for the experience—the feeling of nothingness and shame over our own nothingness. For this reason, falling in love occurs more frequently among young people, since they are profoundly uncertain, unsure of their worth, and often ashamed of themselves. The same thing applies to people of other ages when they lose something in their lives— when their youth ends or when they start to grow old. There is an irreparable loss of something in the self, a feeling that we will inevitably become devoid of value or degraded, compared with what we have been. It isn't the longing for an affair that makes us fall in love, but the conviction that we have nothing to lose by becoming whatever we will become; it is the prospect of nothingness stretching before us. Only then do we develop the inclination for the different and the risky, that propensity to hurl ourselves into all or nothing which those who are in any way satisfied with their lives cannot feel.

Can we identify any other sign or symptom of the predisposition to fall in love? Sometimes it all begins with a profound, radical disappointment in ourselves or in what we have loved. This may be a serious illness, the realization that we have been slighted for a long time, or an accumulation of many, many disappointments that we've always denied. Then we react by becoming melancholy, by withdrawing into ourselves. But we may happen to look around and notice that other people are happy. This is the sign. In general, we don't perceive other people's happiness strongly, viscerally, but when we are inclined to fall in love, we are forced to feel it in an almost painful way, and we envy it. The word "envy" may be misleading: there is rather the sense that we have deliberately been left out, a feeling that we are excluded from a world of intense desires and pleasures. The desires and pleasures that we perceive in others are in fact our own desires and our renewed ability to live intensely. At this point, however, we don't see them as ours; we only recognize them in other people. Thus the world becomes more intense and at the same time more painful, because the individual feels he is excluded from a fuller life that he senses and recognizes, against his will, in other people, the happy ones. In this state, he is eligible only for obligations and self-denial; only by accepting his everyday obligations as an unquestioned imperative does he manage to hold together the fragments of his own embittered ego. So the propensity to fall in love is not revealed in the desire to do so, but in the perception of the vital intensity and happiness of the world, in feeling ourselves excluded, and in envying that happiness while knowing that it is inaccessible.

Then, in this dull everyday routine of obligations, where we move like Calvino's "nonexistent knight," we occasionally feel something like an omen. Sometimes it is an omen of ruin, the sense of an imminent catastrophe that involves the whole world. In this case, too, the conflict that is building inside us seems objective: a disruption of the world, an obscure fear and an attraction to that obscurity. Sometimes, when we are tired or excited, we feel as if we have been seized by a sense of destiny: something grandiose and terrible is about to happen; our words become inspired. This happens in an instant, and then everything returns to the way it was. At other times it is a song that spontaneously comes to mind, or a desire for poetry so eloquent that it seems to beg for an answer. Some people even experience actual visions or fantasies full of obscure or exalting meanings. These are all momentary and uncertain revelations of the "extraordinary," signs of a transcendence of the self, of the worthless self, as if there were another self waiting to appear and be recognized, but seeming to come from an external, objective source. To fall in love is not to desire a beautiful or interesting person; it is a remaking of the social sphere, a vision of the world with new eyes. During the preparation for this experience, the new world begins to appear at certain moments socially distant (the happy ones), at others distant in time (something that will happen). It has still not materialized, but there is already a hierarchy, a distinction of what is important and has value from what is valueless and from our feeling that we lack what is important. There is also an omen of something to come.

The person who wants to fall in love in order to enrich his existence, to add something marvelous to it, isn't able to do so. Only the person whose life is missing something approaches the door that separates the real from the everyday. This is true for every nascent state, and thus for every collective movement. During this preparatory period, the "response" may not come from another person, may not lead to love. If the person who is prepared for this transformation finds himself in a social system where a collective movement is about to erupt, he will find recognition in this. He will not fall in love with another person, but will enter the nascent state of a group.

So it is possible not to fall in love even if we desire it intensely. But if we want to, can we make someone fall in love with us? Yes. This is possible because there is always someone who is ready for love, who is ready to hurl himself into the all or nothing of a new life. He may meet a person who shows him that everything is possible and who is in his eyes the door through which he can reach the fullest freedom and joy. It is possible to cause someone to fall in love if, at the right moment, he meets a person who shows that she understands him profoundly, who encourages him in his desire for renewal, who pushes him in this direction, who gives him confidence, who declares herself willing to share the risk of the future with him, to stand by him forever, no matter what happens. Anyone can cause a person who is waiting for the summons to fall in love if she can make him hear the voice that calls him by name and tells him that his time has come, if she tells him that she is here to recognize the destiny that is his, if she makes out the signs of it on his face, his hands, in what he has done. She makes herself someone who embodies a certainty and calls him to her so that they can move beyond. Then he recognizes himself in her and falls in love.

All this can be done, and in a most beguiling way. Who does it? Who wants to make another person fall in love without being in love himself? First, there is the type of person we have already mentioned, the one who wants to fall in love in order to enrich his everyday life. He searches for a response, is afraid it won't come, and so in his constant attempt at "seduction," gets what he wants from those who have the internal need to give it. But the motive may also be something more shabby, like the desire for success or even the desire for power. Love gives an enormous power to the lover, and this power can be pleasurable because it flatters one's vanity, because it makes the other person into a slave who is always available, always ready for any order, any desire. Then there are those who make someone fall in love with them for money, while others do it for still other reasons.

What happens later, when the other person has fallen in love, when there is one who loves and another who, although loved, is not himself actually in love because he has never loved? This is the extreme case of a one-sided relationship that has become heartless through deception. But precisely because there is deception, it is revealed in the great majority of cases. The experience of falling in love is made up of tests, a series of tests, and whoever has made another person fall in love—because he himself wanted to fall in love, or because he relishes power, or because he wanted someone to be totally available—very quickly grows tired of this series of tests. If nothing else, he grows tired of constantly being asked "Do you love me?" in ways and forms that he can't answer. In all such cases, the tests work, and the deception is revealed. But this doesn't ease the great pain, the desperate loss of the person who was really in love. In the end, however, the more bold, superficial and coarse the deception, the less serious the damage. Hope gives way to the certainty of nothing: "She never loved me; she was never really in love at all; nothing ever happened." The painful experience vanishes like an illusion. Even if the distinction is sometimes difficult to make, we must discriminate between this situation and a relationship in which one person was more in love than the other, but was convinced that the other was in fact in love with him. The case is different here, because we cannot be certain of a deception, and any decision to break off the relationship is made in doubt—a doubt that, when we are in love, appears as a dilemma. I shall return to this point later because the way out is terrible—apathy.

11

WHEN WE FALL IN LOVE WITH SOMEONE, DOES SHE (OR
he) become perfect in our eyes? Some of the things we
have already said lead us to answer "yes," but others do
not. The beloved may become perfect because we find in
her what is most desirable. But she may not become so
because we don't accept all her plans; we shield ourselves
from them and actually struggle against her. At times, we
find a profound truth in what she says to us, a truth we
never could have grasped by ourselves; it is as if she had
given us a new perspective on the world. But this does
not always happen, for at other times we don't agree and
try to explain our point of view at length and convince
her of it. Neither of the lovers is perfect in the other's
eyes; neither is the repository of truth. But each lover,
in the other's eyes, is the way to truth, and when we fall
in love, truth is something that exists and is accessible.
When the other person—through an observation, judgment or story—shows us something that we had not seen
before and didn't even imagine could exist, it is as if she
had opened for us the window through which she looks at
the world. It is her perspective, just as we have our own.
But it isn't an opinion, a "point of view," as we say in the
language of everyday life; it is a *window that opens onto*

the real. She sees from another point of view what we too had observed without seeing and without understanding. Our two perspectives are focused on the same reality, the same truth that is in large part unknown to us, but that nonetheless stands before us and can be grasped and known. One way in which the experience of falling in love differs from everyday life is in the certainty that truth is attainable and that every problem has a solution, even if we have yet to find it. So neither of the two lovers is perfect; neither is infallible. Neither, taken by himself, is an absolute in the other's eyes. But in their meeting—in their ability to see the world from each other's perspective—they realize to the fullest possible extent the capacity to see and understand. This is what comes as close as possible to the truth. The group in the nascent state—be it a couple or a crowd—is thus not the absolute, but the path that leads to it, the way to approach it, the window through which reality is glimpsed. And since when we fall in love all other people are reduced to a single person—the beloved—she becomes the one "through whom" truth is manifested; she is not the repository or guardian of truth, but the door that is now open, now half-closed, now completely closed.

This opening onto the truth of things does not depend on a sublime intelligence or on any extraordinary quality in the beloved. In fact, we sometimes see through her weaknesses or her naïveté. If another person makes certain observations, judgments or appraisals, we don't give them a second thought; we consider them superficial or naïve or simply wrong. When the beloved makes them, our first impression is the same. Then we think about them and grasp their value—from her perspective, on the basis of her experience, of what she sees is true. In doing so, we give value to that experience and that perspective, and we grasp the world through her subjectivity. Since that subjectivity isn't just any subjectivity (the others don't matter at all to us, and we ignore them), we take it as a thing of value and notice that the world is "also" this way. This is the path through which the profound self-understanding we have mentioned occurs; because each lover sees his own authentic perspective recognized, he feels that his own unmistakable and unique subjectivity is deeply appreciated. When we fall in love, what is absolutely individual assumes a universal value; what she sees has the same value as what I see. Yet this is not a source of skepticism, but of certainty: both are perspectives on life which enrich our awareness of it; instead of canceling out each other, they are integrated.

This phenomenon, which is revealed when we fall in love, continues in love itself, losing something and gaining something else. Let us consider the case of two parents who have a mongoloid child. They know that their child is not as intelligent as other children, that when he goes to school, he can't do the same things others can. The parents don't love their child any less for this. In order to love him, though, they can't judge him against the standard of other children; if they did so, they would regard their child as limited, incomplete, insufficient, as someone who has no value. Their love would be love-as-compassion, an act of filling in what is missing. But their experience is different: they grasp and give value to the specific nature of their child's perspective. If he is frightened, bewildered or amazed by something that would be "normal" for another child, they participate in this response and see in it an authentic perspective on the world. It's entirely possible to be amazed by what later in life we have forgotten to look at with amazed eyes! The child's eyes, then, are the eyes of an innocence in regard to the world which others don't have or have lost, and the world is enriched by that gaze. The love of these two parents has made them the guardians of a different (and lost) perspective on the world.

So to fall in love is to open ourselves to the existence of a personal perspective, while to love is to be the guardian of this perspective. Does this mean, then, that we become incapable of judging? No. The parents understand their frightened or amazed child, but they themselves are not frightened or amazed. They know the actual situation, and in spite of their awareness, they love rather than scorn him.

In comparing these experiences, we can find the answer to a theological problem that has arisen countless times in both Islam and Christianity. Can God, who is infinite and omniscient, love man, who is finite and capable only of error? Seen from the point of view of falling in love, the answer can only be "no." A lover cannot admit that his other, his beloved, is inferior to him; she can only be superior, because she is the door through which he arrives at the truth. In this sense, God cannot fall in love with man, who is infinitely inferior to Him. Yet falling in love is also the path through which what is subjective acquires value in itself, and this is the dominant experience in love. When we are in love, each of us is aware of the other's weaknesses, but despite this awareness, we understand, forgive or even appreciate them. We appreciate them, for example, when they are expressions of altruism, generosity or enthusiasm, all of which can cause problems in everyday life, but which on the scale of values are virtues. It follows that God can love man (especially if he is virtuous, which is to say, disinterested). This theological problem confirms the validity of our decision to distinguish between falling in love and love itself, even though we can recognize that many bridges and roads connect them and make love a consequence of falling in love.

12

IT IS OFTEN SAID THAT FALLING IN LOVE BELONGS TO adolescents, to young people. It does not befit the mature man, the married woman with children, the austere politician, the bishop. It is appropriate for movie stars and artists because these people, after all, retain some of the frivolity and irresponsibility of adolescence. Yet not just falling in love, but political fervor, religious enthusiasm and throwing oneself headlong into an adventure are all things connected with youth. So are rapid changes of mood, the rapid shift from enthusiasm to desperation and then back to enthusiasm for something new. So are mystical and political crises, the denunciation of the hypocrisy of the world, the affirmation of absolute justice, the hope for a totally good world and, at the same time, profound disappointment, bitterness, desperation. We find almost all the properties of the nascent state concentrated in adolescence. Adolescence is the time when the nascent state occurs most frequently. And we can understand why: adolescence is the period of transition from childhood and the childhood family to the adult world in all its complexity. If the nascent state is a separation of what was united and a union of what was separated, there is no time like adolescence in which it must bring about such radical

changes in our lives. When we are adolescents, we separate from the family, from the world of childhood values,
emotions and beliefs, and unite with others in love, but
we also join parties and groups, become involved with
politics, acquire knowledge. Adolescence is thus the age of
continual dying and rebirth as something else, of continual experimentation with the frontiers of the possible.
Hence adolescence offers us a rapid succession of new
loves, a continual uniting and separating in a succession of
revelations and disappointments.

When it is said, therefore, that falling in love is suited to
adolescence and youth and not to other ages, nothing pre-
vents us from accepting this as fact. It is also said that
falling in love is inappropriate later on, that it is not good,
that it should not occur. And if it does occur, if the mature
man falls in love, if the woman with children loses her
head, then it is said that they are acting like "kids." They
are doing something unsuited to their age, their circumstances, their responsibilities. What is permitted in adolescence—namely, breaking away from the family—is
prohibited here. In fact, acting like kids when we are older
means this and only this: breaking away from an institution when we should not be doing so. In the case of the
child, it is permitted and recognized; he must do it. But it
should not happen at other ages. The child cannot and
must not remain a child, with his mother and father and
his toys. The adult, however, has "arrived"; he has
achieved a certain *status*, a "position"; he is in a certain
"place" and must stay there. But the nascent state breaks
with the consolidated institution to create another, alter-

native solidarity. It displaces, leads elsewhere, brings death and resurrection. Thus, in whatever form the nascent state appears, as long as it is "child's play" it is tolerated, but it becomes frightening if it happens to an adult. And then the first fundamental mechanism of control is to declare it inappropriate and discredit it by saying precisely that it is "child's play," that the adult is acting like a child.

The institution is horrified by the nascent state. This is the only thing that the institution fears, because it is the only thing that merely by its appearance shakes the institution's very foundations. From the point of view of the institution, the nascent state is, by definition, what was unexpected. Since its logic is different from that of everyday life, it is incomprehensible. Since it attacks institutions in the name of their own values, accusing them of hypocrisy, it is fanaticism. Since it remakes the past and declares bonds and contracts dissolved, it is monstrous. Confronted by the nascent state, even in its most minute form, the institution is shaken in its certainties. Reproducing the event in which the institution is born, revealing the forces that nourish it in their fundamental purity, the nascent state creates a situation of mortal risk. All social mechanisms, all the wisdom of tradition, now have only one aim: to try to suppress it, to render it impossible. Only if this destruction fails will society try to force the nascent state into known and recognized forms. Engagement, separation, divorce, the stereotype of the lover, revenge, marriage—these are all institutional forms for the particular kind of nascent state that we call falling in love.

But they all come later. In the beginning, these possibilities do not exist. Falling in love is not even recognized as such. Faced with the event that should not happen, society always reacts by trying to ensure that it isn't happening, that in fact it never happened. At first society renders the nascent state mute: it describes this experience with terms drawn from everyday life, none of which are appropriate. In doing so, society leads the lovers to define themselves as something they are not, as something other than they are. And if they don't define themselves in these terms, the institution declares their experience madness, a thing devoid of sense, foolishness.

First society derides the nascent state. The grown man in love with a teen-age girl is grotesque, ridiculous. Crying about it is particularly grotesque, because tears are only for children, for the powerless, not for someone who has a definite status, a place in society. A barrier of winking and ridicule is formed around the person in love. He is doing something that isn't serious; he has lost his seriousness. What for him is a dramatic, essential event is considered even by his dearest friends as frivolity, stupidity, a childish act. "Don't act like a child," his friends tell him. The psychologist pronounces the lover's behavior regressive, infantile, or is ready with another, diametrically opposed interpretation: it is pure sexuality, repressed sexuality, a sexual outlet. Falling in love is reduced to sexuality because sexual desire does not have a single, exclusive object; hence it is less frightening. When it later becomes clear that the relationship is strong, society says that the lover sees in his beloved an absolute perfection without defects, without uncertainties, portraying him as delirious. In reality, the relationship that occurs when we fall in love is a process, a finding and a losing. The beloved is at once constant and precarious, unique and different, empirical and ideal.

At the same time, society declares that the lover's affection will certainly not be returned. "You poor deluded girl," say her friends or parents, "he will leave you just as he left that other woman." If the new love is mutual, however, another distortion is ready: the lovers are tied to each other; they live in an isolated universe, alone, shut up in their egotism. And yet love is a joyous opening of ourselves to the world, which appears beautiful and happy; it is an opening of ourselves to others, who we feel are our friends. After having described the lovers as united, society contradicts itself and calls them pseudolovers, people who are not in love (their experience is a caprice, an infatuation, a romantic exaggeration and so on).

Everyday life also tries to impose its dichotomies: either you love forever or you don't love at all; either the beloved is an absolute or she is like everyone else; either the lovers are always together or they are always apart. Through these definitions and interrogations, society forces the lovers to define themselves in a contradictory, insane way. This situation becomes more dramatic when we consider the conflict of values it can bring about. Falling in love is an act of liberation. And freedom means not only an independence from bonds, but also the right to be independent from the consequences of past decisions made by ourselves or others. In reality, the past is not totally denied in the nascent state; it is denied in order to be transcended in a new synthesis. Many things from the past actually acquire new values. Institutional culture categorically affirms this point: a promise is a promise, a contract a contract; a contract cannot be broken at whim. The fact is that falling in love is not a whim; it is the discovery that there were two elements in contracts made in the past—one that could be imposed through the will, another that had meaning only when it was spontaneous. "Will you love this man in sickness and in health?" the contract asks. By saying "yes," each person can pledge to love and help the other. But each cannot pledge "to be in love, to love passionately, desperately." The person in love denounces the hidden part of the contract and says: "I hold firm to my practical promises, but no one can swear by his feelings. Authenticity is more important than fiction; I can't lie. When I made the contract, I swore not to lie." So he denounces the contract on the basis of the principles implied in it, the higher values from which any action derives its worth. This is so true that he is ready to pay with his life. Inevitably, the conflict becomes more serious and shifts to this level. There is always a moment when it is posed in terms of all or nothing, life or death.

The person who falls in love comes from a world of rules, certainties, clearly defined paths, prohibitions. At this point, his life proceeds completely according to habit. He acts, but he no longer really knows in his heart why he acts. He does not have an authentic will. He acts because other people ask him to, because there are rules and responsibilities. He carries out these responsibilities in an increasingly laborious way. Then, through a transformation, he realizes that he was lying to himself, that he was lying to others, that his life was a constant falsification of reality. The institution asks him to continue this falsification because it is interested in his observable behavior. To use the theological language of Protestantism, the institution is interested in works, not faith. In the nascent state, however, works alone, if they are not authentically willed, have no value; they are false, hypocritical. But the institution is not interested in intentions, only in actions, facts, things; it treats feelings and values as objects, as things. When I say "the institution," I mean all those who are not in the nascent state. The abandoned wife or husband, the fiancée or lover asks him (or her) to stay. They know very well that they cannot say, "Be in love with me; love me passionately." So they tell him, "Give up the other person and stay with me." They are interested in his physical presence, his being here, his not having the other person. The pain and desperation that the person in love is experiencing don't interest them. "I prefer to have you near me, desperate, crying all through the night, rather than lose you." In a word, neither your feelings nor your happiness interests me; I am interested in you only as a thing. Hegel calls this attitude *reification;* Marx describes it as commodification.

This is the face that the institution turns toward the nascent state. It is a terrible, inhuman face of which the institution itself is unaware. The institution, in fact, also springs from the nascent state. We shall see later how love, the pact and marriage spring from the experience of falling in love. At a certain point, the nascent state comes to an end and the institution takes its place. In that transition, the institution declares that it completely puts into practice the experience of the nascent state. The Mass is the reproduction of the sacrifice of the Cross. The catechism says that the Mass is actually the sacrifice itself. But those who attend the Mass either may or may not relive the experience. A mystic relives it, but a distracted person does not, because he is thinking of something else. A person who does not believe observes the Mass as a spectacle, more or less strange, more or less boring. The Mass, which in the nascent state from which it was born was the reliving of the sacrifice of the Cross (and is so again when that nascent state is reactivated), continues to reactivate it as an institution without the participation of men. All celebrations, holidays, contracts and institutions are born—and reborn—through movements composed of real men. But insofar as institutions have no need of men's consent, they do not need men. If the institution is not constantly revitalized by the nascent state, it becomes inhuman and reduces men to things. And it is in this form that the nascent state encounters the institution. Since the nascent state is the truth of the institution—falling in love is the truth of love—it sees the institution as devoid of truth, as pure power. And since the institution cannot see its own truth in the nascent state—which is precarious, fleeting, pure becoming—it sees that state as irrationality, madness, scandal.

13

HOW DO WE PASS FROM FALLING IN LOVE TO LOVE IT-
self? Through a series of tests—tests that we administer to
ourselves and to the other person and that are imposed on
us by the external situation. Some of these tests are crucial. If they are passed, falling in love enters the routine of
everyday certainties that we call love. If these tests are not
passed, love is replaced by something else: rejection, apathy or estrangement.

However things turn out, the tests are generally forgotten. When we pass from falling in love to love itself, the
tests appear trivial to us in retrospect, almost a game. In
our memory, the movement to love occurs as the spaces of
everyday life are gradually filled with our devotion and
care for the other person. Our enthusiasm is gently extinguished in loving devotion to him (or her). In reality,
however, this serenity is always the product of dramatic
events whose outcome is unknown until the last moment.

But the tests are also forgotten when we don't move beyond falling in love—that is, when either person or both
fail to pass the tests that are put to them. In this case, we
don't recall that we imposed the tests, only that the other
person did not love us enough, meaning that in reality he
did not love us at all.

So, when the tests are passed, we project back in time, through our memory, the continuity of the love we are living in the present. When they are not passed, we project back the continuity of our present disaffection.

Falling in love, however, is a series of tests. First of all, there are the tests we give ourselves: *the proofs of truth.* When we fall in love, a typical experience is the one in which we become "sated" with the other person. Falling in love is also a resistance to love, an unwillingness to yield to the existential risk of putting ourselves completely in the other person's hands. So we search for the beloved, but we also want to do without her. Often, in happy moments, we tell ourselves, "I have reached the utmost happiness I will ever be able to achieve; now I can lose her and return to the way I was before, keeping only the memory of it. I have gotten what I wanted; it's enough." To achieve the maximum that is possible and then do without it—this is the fantasy of satiety. In a certain sense, we can abandon ourselves totally only because we think that this time will be the last. But this is the way we test ourselves, for after a separation occurs we notice that desire returns and that we continue to love, to desire desperately, and we need another "last time." The "last time" thus becomes a new beginning and the necessity for a new beginning. With each "last time," we fall in love again, and the beloved is impressed on us as the only authentic object of eros. It is a struggle against ourselves which we lose, and we must surrender. Yet the fact that we must surrender does not prevent the struggle from taking place or from being real. Our separation, which is real, also has real effects on the beloved, because she feels that we want to detach ourselves. And since she too is testing herself, the two moments of detachment may coincide. In this case, longer periods of separation occur, in which we may perform many actions that later may cause the other person to be jealous or may be considered proof that we don't love her.

In order to detach ourselves, we look for reasons. We look to the other person's behavior for everything that will justify us in our detachment: we look for signs that she does not truly love us, that she does not love us as much as we love her; we seek reasons for not believing that she will love us in the future. All these things indicate our fear of giving ourselves over to the other person without any guarantee of reciprocity. The very fact that the other's love appears to us as unmerited "grace" is frightening, because that grace might not be there at the very moment when we desire it most and can't do without it. Therefore we want to do without that grace, or we try to transform it into certainty, the certainty of reciprocity. We look in the other person's actions for proof that she loves us; we examine them as signifiers of the reciprocity of love: "Does she need me as much as I need her?" The other person's behavior is analyzed in this light so that we can know what she is and what she will be. The test "she loves me, she loves me not" is applied to the other person's behavior, rather than to the petals of a daisy: "If she does this, it means . . .; if she doesn't do this, it means . . ." This is done with the simplest things, such as whether she arrives early or late, or whether or not she looks at another person. But the meaning is never clear. What does it mean if she arrives late, panting? That she forgot about me, or that she made an effort to reach me and therefore her lateness is proof of her love? On the other hand, even when the proof is negative, an explanation, a look or a caress from her is enough to make us forget it, to reassure us. Her sincerity is proved if it is experienced as sincerity.

I have called all these proofs of truth. We don't establish them to elicit a certain behavior: they are tests addressed to ourselves so we can know whether or not we love—that is, so we can know the truth. But there is another class of tests that are true and proper demands made on the other person, tests in which we ask her to change, to do things she would not have done. These are *proofs of reciprocity*. When we fall in love, we reorganize around the beloved all our previous feelings, our work, our entire life. To want together the things that each person authentically wants signifies the need for change, for separating ourselves from things that we wanted before, things to which we gave importance. What will be integrated into the new love and what will be separated from it are not at all decided beforehand; they are the result of a continuous reciprocal exploration. Each person wants to integrate as much as possible into his love, and he develops a *plan* that does not coincide with the other person's. Each of us asks the other to recognize our plan. Thus "Do you love me?" also means "Do you agree to enter my plan?" And when the other person asks, "Do you love me?" she is asking in turn, "But do you agree to enter mine?" "I love you" means "I modify my plan; I approach it from your perspective; I accept your request; I give up something that I wanted; I want what you want along with you." Yet at the same time I ask, "Do you love me?" meaning, "What are you changing? What are you giving up?" "Do you love me?" therefore is always a request for something I want, a renunciation of something you want. "Do you love me?" is the request to take me with all the weight of my concreteness and my restrictions and to renounce your restrictions. The plan that each of us makes for ourselves involves the other person: it is also a life plan for her; it is the proposal of what we both have to want together.

But there are things that both lovers don't want, incompatible things. Some of the more trivial ones can be renounced easily, others can be deferred, but others are essential. In this sense, the search for what has to be wanted by both lovers involves a continuous creation and revision of plans, a continuous search for other paths. But it is also a continuous discovery of points that cannot be denied, because if they are not realized, love itself loses meaning: they are the *points of no return*. In the plans that are created and revised, these essential points always reappear, like indissoluble knots which the lover must accept, make his own, insert structurally into his plan, because otherwise there is no real place for me with all the richness of my life. He says he loves me, but in reality, there is no place for the real me in his imaginary world. There is an essential part of me which asks to be recognized and accepted. But he avoids it: he wants me to renounce it, to yield to him, losing myself, losing the profound sense of my wanting to be new and different, alive. He says he loves me, for example, but he doesn't bring me into his life. He keeps me apart from his work. When he travels, he doesn't travel with me. He wants to confine me to the role of the lover whom he sees every so often, the silent lover whom he loves in the shadows. He continues to be himself, doesn't put his relationships in jeopardy, maintains all of them. I have to be only his secret refuge, have to reduce my life to waiting for him to come, when he wants, according to the rules that he himself lays down. No, this isn't acceptable; for me, this isn't living. For another woman, it may be so; it would have been so for me too, but not now. Now I want a full life. So I ask him at certain times: "Can I come with you?" My question is a test. If he says "no," it means that he drives me back to the point where I cannot exist.

For him, on the other hand, the problem is symmetrical and inverted. The system of relations in which he is inserted is constructed with a balance that is delicate, sheltered, adjusted. Any abrupt shift may make it explode. He needs time to reorganize things slowly, to change his job, to locate the right place in his life for certain people, to be able to take care of his children in a new way. In his new love he finds the strength to revise his life plan: it is a refuge from which he leaves strengthened, secure. Thanks to this love, he finds the strength to modify himself and reality. In fact, he has already begun a new job, has moved to a new city, has developed new habits and begun to make explanations; gradually, he will be free and available, but in order to be so, he needs certainties, he needs love. Yet a decisive act is demanded of him, a sharp break with the past, a total throwing of himself into the new with the danger of losing everything that he loves and that he wants to reorganize around the new center of his life, his new love. But if he loses everything, the center also remains empty. He will be able to bring to the meeting only a mutilated, incomplete self, composed of nostalgia and a sense of guilt. He is all the things that he is, and he cannot abandon any of them without ceasing to be what he is.

Every lover has encountered a point of no return: every lover asks the other to renounce some essential thing, a thing that has been rendered essential precisely by the new love that wants to reorder around itself life in all its richness. Every lover asks the other to renounce an essential part of himself, what renders him fully capable of loving. In a word, each of us asks the other person to destroy his concrete humanity, to dehumanize himself.

In theological language, God gives Abraham the test of dehumanization. He will have to kill what he loves most, his first-born son, Isaac. This is the dilemma, the choice between two things that make any choice impossible because they both involve dehumanization. The movement from falling in love to love itself requires loving someone who asks you to become a criminal. To love means to trust someone who acts in such a way that it is objectively absurd to love him. The movement from falling in love to love requires each of us to prove that we are capable of being loved even though we are dehumanized. The proof (of reciprocity) is a struggle in which each of us asks the other for an unconditional surrender, the loss of his concrete humanity, the only humanity he knows. It is a struggle between people who love one another, but it also is always a fight to the death. The imagery of love must not deceive us. Whoever undergoes this test resists it desperately. And whoever gives the test gives it sincerely, and decides in his heart that if the other person does not pass it, she will no longer be the beloved. Each of us wants to be loved, even though we appear inhuman and say "no"; each of us wants to be loved, even though we impose inhuman tests as a condition of saying "yes." But the test is always reciprocal. In the Bible, God tests Abraham, but at the same time, Abraham tests his God. What would happen to God, in fact, if Abraham killed his son? He would no longer be a God of love, but a cruel, bloody God. Moses is also put to the test by his God when he is asked to hurl himself into the waters of the Red Sea. At that instant, however, God too is put to the test because He cannot ask this and then allow the waters to drown His people. A God who acts in this way would be a deceiver, a devil.

The key to the solution lies in the fact that the point of no return is requested but not required; it is a check signed but not cashed. Abraham is about to kill his son, but God does not require the sacrifice. Both of them have passed the test. Both have withstood the proof, and both have accomplished an essential renunciation; both have encountered and acknowledged an insuperable limit. Love becomes possible only when the other person's point of no return is taken as one's own authentic limit, is desired as one's own authentic limit.

When this happens, *the pact* is reached. Each of us

knows that the other person will not ask us what he cannot ask. This certainty, discovered in desperation, constitutes the firm point of reciprocal trust: it is *the institution of reciprocity.* I know that I love, and I cannot avoid loving; I know that I have a limit that I cannot avoid, and I accept it.

Thus love emerges from an *institution,* a pact. And the pact emerges from a limit, from the recognition that not everything is possible, that the impossible exists. In this way, love is always love of what was not wanted, an alternative life that we opposed.

The process I have described does not happen only once, but many times; and every time it encounters desperation and ends in a pact. The new certainties become the point of departure for reorganizing our daily existence.

There are no rules for knowing whether falling in love becomes love. There are no rules for knowing whether or not the dilemma is insoluble. Our life plans can be so different that they may not admit compromise. Every lover requires the dehumanization of the beloved: if he obtains it, he loses her; if he does not, he loses her all the same. This loss is more probable the greater the difference, and the greater the difference, the more disruptive the experience of falling in love. Disruptive in fact means that many things must be upset, reorganized or revised. The most intense love is the one in which the most existence, the most wealth of experience, the most responsibility and the most life are at stake. Falling in love is a revolution: the more complex, articulate and rich the order is, the more terrible the disruption, the more difficult, dangerous and risky the process. Often two people fall in love with each other, and one of them brings a great wealth of experience, while the other brings a great possibility for change, since he has fewer ties. This is frequently the case with a married person and an unmarried one, an adult and a young person, a (politically or religiously) committed person and one who has no commitments. The person who has more ties, more obligations, more things to integrate and change is the one for whom falling in love is more disruptive. But the other person loves him for this very complexity, which gives density and meaning to his capacity for change, for planning a new existence—and to his desire for power. However, it is precisely this diversity, precisely its disruptive nature that is difficult to transform into a stable love, into a serene and lasting life together. It is easier for love to exist when two people are in a more balanced situation, each one having few ties (like young adults or adolescents), or when they have already broken many ties. But in this case, paradoxically, the experience of falling in love is also less intense because its revolutionary task is smaller; at times, it has almost nothing to revolutionize. In this sense, falling in love is perfectly analogous to the great collective movements. There are collective movements that involve a social system from top to bottom, that rend it with terrible wars without resulting in the emergence of a new, more stable power. There are, on the other hand, movements that end in a short time with the seizure of power. The Protestant Reformation was a profound movement that involved all of Europe, but there was no seizure of a Bastille or a Winter Palace. In the same way, falling in love can brand and profoundly disrupt the existence of one or two people without creating love. On the other hand, love can emerge without a disturbing experience of falling in love, from a quiet meeting, from the pleasure of being together, from the ability to establish easily that mutual desire for what each person wants and the pact which makes that desire an institution.

Falling in love, like every nascent state, is an exploration of the possible starting from the impossible; it is an attempt to impose the imaginary on existence. The greater the task, the longer the journey and the less likely the arrival. The history of falling in love, then, amounts to the history of that journey and its hardships, the struggles endured, without an arrival or a happy landing.

14

WHEN WE FALL IN LOVE, WE GENERALLY FEEL NO JEAL-
ousy. What does it mean, then, when jealousy appears?
When we fall in love, we discover something that is worth
more than anything else, and we love and want it in its individuality, in the details of its existence. To feel that our
love is returned means to realize that what we are has
value, however poor we have judged ourselves in comparison with others. We have value because the one we
love, the person who incarnates every potential value,
gives it to us. None of us imagines that he is the most
beautiful or intelligent person in the world. None of our
virtues, measured against the world, makes us preferable
to other people. Set against any criterion of worldly value,
what we are is always inferior. And yet we love and appreciate ourselves because we feel that deep down *there is
some value in us, an irreplaceable uniqueness.* When we
fall in love, this uniqueness is recognized. When another
person loves us, she loves this unmistakable uniqueness of
ours. Even when she asks us to change, she recognizes our
uniqueness, and the change that she asks for is only a new
blossoming of that uniqueness, a flowering, a transition
from potentiality to action. Just as we find some detail in
the beloved—the fold of her mouth, her scent or the per-

fume she uses, the shape of her breasts, the curve of her thighs, her hands, her glance, a certain dress, the things that please her, the books she reads—so she finds something in us that symbolizes every beautiful thing. And this makes us happy. If the person we love appreciates other things as well, like traveling or staying at home, reflection or talking, we try to appreciate and share them with her.

Jealousy is the interruption of this process, its overturning from the outside. A jealous person is one who notices (whether rightly or wrongly doesn't matter at this point) that his beloved finds in someone else the same sort of thing that he finds in her: a detail or a gesture, an ability or a quality. Someone else amuses her or knows how to make her happy: he is handsome, young or intelligent. Jealousy presents itself as the discovery that the person we love is attracted or fascinated by something that we don't have, but that someone else does. We are never jealous of a thing, an animal or a profession, only another person—a person who in our eyes has something that exerts an irresistible fascination on the one we love, an irresistible fascination just like the one that she has for us and that we, if she loved us deeply, would have for her. Jealousy is discovering that our beloved depends for the realization of her desires on something that another person possesses, but that we do not; another person, not we, has at his disposal something that has value for her. Jealousy also reveals itself as a weakness in the one we love, a weakness with respect to things that should not have value, but that are valuable for her. She loves cars, for example, and is fascinated by drivers. I, who am not a driver, who discovered precisely through my love that being a driver has no value (and cannot have value because I am not one), find my relationship overturned. Her attraction to something that I don't have, something that should not have value, degrades what I am and completely annihilates my value. Our love is invaded by something external, by an alien power that annihilates our criteria of value. It therefore cancels out this love as a mutual relationship. Hence jealousy cannot exist when both lovers fall in love, because there can be nothing, on the outside, capable of exerting an attraction of this kind. The external world consists of passing facts, and these cannot prevail over the real; the ephemeral cannot prevail over being. Jealousy can of course arise as a doubt, as a crack that widens in moments of separation, especially as a justification for our wanting to separate. "It isn't worth trying; she wants other things; I have nothing to give her." But this doubt is quickly resolved by mutual recognition. In the nascent state, there cannot be any external value superior to those of the lover and the beloved. When there is a mutual love, the beloved's interests, her enthusiasm for things, her kindness to others, her success become qualities that render her worthy of love, that confirm her value and hence also the value of her sincerity, her transparency, her being what she is. It is only when that activity, those meetings with other people, that success prevent the union of life plans, become signals of a difference in plans, that they acquire a negative significance. But even in this case there is no jealousy. There is sadness, because we feel slighted, because our requests are not satisfied, because the future appears impractical to us, because we must decide to change. But we are not jealous; rather, we are about to begin the tests we discussed in the preceding chapter.

If jealousy appears after we fall in love, it means that one of the lovers really does not want to love the other or is not in love. If the jealousy is unmotivated—because the other person is really in love—then it signifies our fear, our desire not to love, not to yield, not to open ourselves to the trust of the nascent state. The beloved really does not find anything irresistible in others; they have no power over her. We think they do because we have no faith in our own ego; we don't believe in the value of our own individuality. We, not the beloved, make comparisons between ourselves and the world; we, not the beloved, accept as the criterion of value what belongs to nonvalue and the realm of the ephemeral. There are those who are so uncertain of themselves, who find life such a painful trial, that they cannot believe they are valuable as individuals. They share in the extraordinary experiences of the nascent state, but they don't believe that they can be the object of these experiences. Grace falls on others, only on others. When we are jealous, we recognize only in others what we cannot recognize in ourselves.

But as we have seen, there is also the case of the one-sided relationship, when one person has really fallen in love and the other has not. Whoever is not in love can then be attracted by someone else, by something that this other person has and that the lover does not. Yet even in this case the person in love is not jealous at the beginning. Since he is in the nascent state, he cannot understand that another person may have something endowed with value in his beloved's eyes: for him, the world remains incidental. He feels that the beloved is attracted by something that does not have value, that she wants something worthless. But precisely because it has no value, he does not care about it much, and he tends to ignore it until the moment he faces the only problem that counts: "Does she love me or not?" If these things are important to her, if that person is indispensable to her, if she prefers him to me, then it means that she doesn't love me. She may have affection for me; my company, my body or my intelligence may please her. But she doesn't love me. The force of the nascent state is still very much alive. He does not doubt the quality of his love or of himself; he doubts the quality of her love and must decide whether to continue loving her without hope or try not to love her, try to detach himself from her, knowing that he still loves her, and hence try to confront the terrible loss of the object of his love—which is *psychic suicide*.

First he will try to fight, to win her with fascination, with song, with utter devotion and self-sacrifice, changing himself in every way. But when he realizes that she does not love him, he can only raise the sword of separation. The force that is still his allows him to cut off the hands that reach toward the beloved and blind the eyes that look everywhere for her. Gradually, in order to stop wanting her, he will have to find reasons to fall out of love; he will have to try to remake what he has lived, investing everything that was with hatred. The hatred will be his attempt to destroy the past, but it is a powerless hatred. At this point, the past has become "what was," inaccessible to the will. Once he has chosen to abandon his love, the extraordinary forces of the nascent state instantly stop operating. He has committed the absolute offense of destroying the foundation of every value, every hope. Now every desire in him subsides, and his ego, which has lost its metaphysical dimension, is pushed back into the universe of appearances. Nothing has value any more; nothing has meaning. In acting, he can only copy other people's gestures, everyday gestures, just as he sees them; he can only repeat what he knows, feel sentiments that he has learned, speak words devoid of content: this is *apathy*. The only real, profound feeling that has the painful character of authenticity is *nostalgia*, the nostalgia for a lost reality. And in order to protect himself from nostalgia, he is forced to fight against the past, to nurture resentment and hatred in himself. He had known the good, the life that says "yes"; then evil lay only in not being. Now he must *construe evil as being*, the life that says "no," the power of the negative.

And here we arrive at the final problem. Will someone who has fallen in love be more deeply hurt if the person he loves tells him that she loves (or simply likes) someone else, or if she says that she really loves no one in particular, but that she prefers her friends to him? Certainly, the latter will be more painful. Indeed, we must not forget that the distinctive structure of the nascent state is the same even if the object of love is another person. Thus the lover instantly recognizes himself in another person in

love, even if she leaves him for someone else. He profoundly understands her love and respects it, no matter
how much pain he may feel. His own experience of falling
in love allows him to understand, to be sympathetic, to
want her to be happy. The event by which he loses her
has the character of a metaphysical necessity for him. He
knows that there is no will at stake any more. He will now
think of suicide as a way to free himself and his beloved of
an intolerable burden. Yet if there are other people who
are dear to him, he will decide to live, devoting himself to
those he loves. Faced with the impossibility of giving
birth to something new, of obtaining something for himself, he will try to give these people some of the life that
he has enjoyed. At this time, he is still experiencing the
extraordinary energy of the nascent state; although he
feels the anguish of the impossible, he also has in himself
an extraordinary impulse for giving. He wants those who
have fallen in love to be happy and withdraws to allow
them to achieve happiness; he wants those who love to be
happy and gives himself to them. This extraordinary
force allows him to perform the ultimate heroic act: *to
give someone else the source of his own life and hope.*
Later, this extraordinary energy will disappear, and apathy will set in.

Yet there is also the case in which the beloved suddenly
tells him, "Instead of making love to you, I want to make
love to the first person who comes by." What is damaged
now is the very foundation of his love and worth. The
soul is invaded by an infinite sadness because everything
that has value is denied, and everything that does not have

value is exalted. Confronted by these two worlds, that of reality, of being, and that of appearance, the beloved chooses the world of appearance, degrading and insulting her lover. What was sacred is turned against the sacred and commits the most infamous sacrilege. No love can end in a worse way than this, because after the painful periods of hatred and apathy, there can be no nostalgia for the beloved, only for the state of love as something debased by someone who will always be unworthy.

Jealousy—the inability to give the one we love something that another person can give her—is the more likely the greater the distance between two people, the more different their worlds and habits. But there are some cases in which jealousy appears because at the very moment that two people fall in love, there is a limitation that neither of them can overcome. This happens in homosexual love, for example. The phenomenology of homosexual love is exactly the same as that for heterosexuality. The distinctive features of the nascent state are entirely identical. Because the experience of falling in love is the same for every sexual preference, we may read a piece of writing about love and not know whether it is homosexual or heterosexual. The very beautiful essay by Roland Barthes, who was himself a homosexual, takes its examples and its language from the universal literature on love and speaks directly to any person in love.* When homosexuals fall in love, however, there is something that makes the passage to the institution, to love itself, more difficult: the resistance and

* Roland Barthes, *A Lover's Discourse*, trans. Richard Howard (New York: Hill and Wang, 1978).

scorn of society and culture. Heterosexuality is a recognized form of behavior. Society provides, at least in some situations, certain institutions to assure the transition to love—the engagement, for example. This does not happen with homosexuality, which is more harshly scorned and even more harshly reduced to pure animal sexuality. Cultural pressure is so strong that homosexuals themselves are traditionally very ashamed to talk about falling in love and often resort to an irritating use of vulgar language as a defense mechanism. But the most profound reason why the homosexual experience of falling in love is more difficult, more spasmodic and, in not a few cases, more tormented by jealousy is that it cannot become the stable love of a couple through having a child. It is an erotic experience that precludes having children. Of course, each of the lovers may have a child with a person of the opposite sex. The thing is that the homosexual always feels this danger, this jealousy, in the background. Remember that homosexuality, especially among the young, is often a brief experience. The one who loves the young person feels that his beloved may one day desire a member of the opposite sex and in particular want a child that he is unable to give. Cultural pressure, the fact that the homosexual in the end is always ambushed by the opposite sex, that he is not able to give his lover a child, mean that homosexuality often tends to remain in the nascent state without managing to become a more serene, lasting love. Thus the homosexual experience of falling in love contains a note of anxiety, of sadness, which is sometimes capable of inspiring very beautiful poetry.

15

MANY PEOPLE BELIEVE THAT THEY HAVE FALLEN IN love when they have not in fact done so. They may have a strong erotic interest in someone, may think constantly about her, may spend happy hours with her and then, after a while, may lose this interest because in the end she has satisfied it. Or they may become attached to a person and desire her intensely because other people admire her. The possibility of being loved, of actually being preferred, entices them, makes them feel a desire and an intoxication that they call love. At times, the cause is disappointment: a love poisoned by jealousy and disappointment makes them search for a substitute, someone with whom to experience a new love. At other times, it is the desire for power or success, the desire to be admired and envied as the companion of a rich or powerful person. In some cases, it is the need to escape boredom and banality. Vacations are especially effective in creating a different and extraordinary opportunity. Yet although they set the stage for an extraordinary experience, that experience remains linked to a particular time and place. The person we admired and adored during a vacation appears out of place and drab when we return to our everyday lives. The experience of falling in love is a revolution of our everyday structural order, not a vacation from it. In other cases, the extraordinary appears in the form of someone who comes from faraway and stays for a little while. Since it is certain that she will leave, quite like someone we may meet on vacation, our love has a "deadline," and we know that the thing will not last forever.

We could multiply these examples. But they concern us only as reasons why certain people become disaffected so easily. In reality, they were never in love. They used the language of love and passion, of the nascent state, in order to enrich and enjoy an experience that would have otherwise been insipid. This kind of "love" has the same relationship to falling in love that a holiday has to a revolution. A holiday is characterized by excess, by the disruption of everyday activity, by transgression; it is permeated by a sense of the exceptional and the extraordinary. Yet what distinguishes a holiday from a revolution is that the former does not overturn the social structure. Everything that is a risk in the revolution is foreseen and calculated in the holiday. The holiday has a predetermined beginning and end; it has tested rules. Everything that happens unfolds within institutional limits. The holiday is an "as if"; it cannot disturb the social structure. When a holiday ends, it is completely over. In the same way, we often hear people say that they have fallen in love with one person and then with another, that they fall in love every month, every year. In reality, in life, the experience of falling in love, like every radical transformation, can happen only a few times; sometimes it never happens at all.

This proliferation of the word "love" also explains why relationships in which one person loves more deeply than the other are so frequent. Almost always in these cases a person who is really in love, who therefore really enters the nascent state, meets another who hurls himself into the adventure because of an erotic attraction, admiration, revenge, disappointment, prestige, jealousy, vacation or some other motive, but without the preconditions for falling in love. We have already said, moreover, that the nascent state has the capacity to communicate its enthusiasm and its language to other people. The person who has fallen in love, in other words, gives his language to the beloved and draws her into his state. In this way, the illusion of being in love is reinforced in her. The person who is really in love, since he acts spontaneously and truly, tends to attribute his own spontaneous and totally sincere behavior to the beloved. If she wants to stay in the game, she can do so. She need only be affectionate and tell little white lies. It is so easy to reassure someone who has really fallen in love! Precisely because the person who is not in love is less spontaneous and more controlled, precisely because she guides and manipulates things, she is in a position to grasp all the lover's weaknesses, his awkward attempts at pleasure, his naïveté. This person does not see the lover with the transfigured eyes of love, but with the cold, clear eyes of everyday life. Those excesses of passion, that desperate tension, that constant need for reassurance and, at the same time, that incredible cruelty seem childish exaggerations and evidence of immaturity to the person who is not in love. The lover, who constantly revises his own past and constantly changes, exploring the range of possibilities, impresses the other person as superficial and not very solid. His crises seem like hysteria to her; his dilemma suggests that he does not know what he wants, that he has a weak character.

And if the lover is a creative spirit, the products of his imagination, in which existence is constantly transformed into fantasies, symbols or poetry, seem like megalomania and artifice to the other person. In a word, the person who is not in love finds the lover inconstant, uncertain, anxious, credulous, exaggerated, egotistic and, in the end, insincere. If she cares for him, she will propose her life plan in a straightforward way, ignore his doubts and dilemmas, and consider his versions of these things morbid daydreams. She gets annoyed, criticizes him, asks him to make a clear choice and not waste time with idle chatter. Meanwhile she conceals her real thoughts and doubts from him; she acts as if he might come to his senses again. In the end, when she finds him too boring or too dramatic, she looks for excuses to criticize him and accuses him of neglecting her or of not being able to understand her. On this basis, she eventually tells him that the thing can't go on because she doesn't feel that she is loved the way she wants to be, and so she looks for someone who can "truly" love her. This is the most common form of "falling out of love": the revelation that something never existed.

But there are also cases in which a mutual relationship actually began. Here the person who becomes disaffected is the one who had silently developed his own plan, had administered several "tests," still in silence, and had considered the other person's demands tests as well. Since everything was conducted in *silence*, the other person did not understand its significance. As a result, she went beyond the point of no return and appeared to be a criminal, someone who, while loving another, has removed herself from his love. By "silence" I mean not only the lover's failure to discuss the nature of his plan and doubts and his concealment of his thoughts, but especially his decision not to reveal his *desperation* when the point of no return was reached. Anyone who loves, in fact, notices that the one she loves has encountered a point of no return because of his desperation. And then she goes no further. But there are those who think their own feelings are a weakness. To reveal their own anguish, their own desperation, means to put themselves at the mercy of the other person. So when a point of no return is reached, they don't speak, explain, beg or despair. The other person then does not understand, and there is really no way she can. May we say that this absence of trust, this fear of showing his own feelings, is a sign that the person in question was not in the nascent state? It certainly reveals a strong resistance to abandoning himself to this state, a need for certainties and security which has little to do with falling in love. But personal experiences, disappointments and sometimes the lack of opportunity also play a part. Everyone tries to protect himself from falling in love; here the defense is just more persistent and achieves its aim.

In this case, then, the tests are painful and sincere. The other person's failure of the tests leads to the lover's hatred, apathy, nostalgia. But this situation is diametrically opposite to the one described in the previous chapter. The

other person, in fact, continues to love her reticent lover.
Every time he feels totally empty, he hears the sound of
her words, her letters reach him, and he experiences her
kindness, which is painful, but always there, helpful, anxious. He can always take a step backward and ease his
pain. If he is lonely, he can endure it more easily because
the other person continues to love him and constantly
gives him proofs of her love. These are insufficient, no
doubt, because in his heart he has already decided what
he wants, but they are nonetheless always pleasant. He no
longer loves because he no longer trusts her, but it gives
him pleasure to feel that he is loved, and especially that he
has power over another person. It is an enormous power
with which he forces her to accept him as he is, a power
with which he can humble her and free himself from his
past, as he prepares himself to search for other things, to
see other things, even a new love. Thus he uses the other
person's love, a sincere, profound and gradually more desperate love, to strengthen himself until he no longer needs
it. This, in essence, is what "falling out of love" is really
like. The attempt to separate succeeds, the tests have already been administered, and the solitary decision to
abandon is made. The separation from the other person
occurs while she is present, while she is still in love. A
bitterly powerful revenge is exercised against this unpro-
tected person, and with great ease, because she is enor-
mously patient. When, in despair, she understands and
breaks off the relationship, she will experience a total apathy. But the one who has "fallen out of love" will be free.

16

ALTHOUGH FALLING IN LOVE IS THE ARRIVAL OF THE extraordinary, it can end in banality. Remember that it is the need for fusion and individuation at the same time; it is a search for what is essential to both lovers, but their two individual plans are different, and they clash. Falling in love thrives on this tension between two different persons who must become one. Falling in love forces the lovers to change precisely because they are different and because they desire to expand their personalities to the fullest in order to realize what they desire most deeply and, at the same time, achieve it together. Falling in love is a search for the meaning of our own destiny. In this uneasy merger of plans, one of the lovers may already have something within him that he had previously tried to realize but without success. When he tries again, the anxieties, the defense mechanisms, the fears that he already felt revive in him. He wants what he wants, but at the same time, he is afraid and tries to protect himself with every precaution. He wants the other person's difference because this is actually what attracts him, insofar as it opens the way to a new life, but at the same time, he tries to limit this difference to reassure himself. This eruptive vitality frightens him; he wants it, but he would like it to be restrained.

Whenever we fall in love, the other person always appears rich with a superabundant life. In fact, she is the incarnation of life in her self-creation, in her energy, the way toward a place where we have never been but desire to be. In this sense, the beloved is always a vital force— free, unforeseeable, polymorphous. She is like a marvelous wild animal, extraordinarily beautiful and extraordinarily alive, an animal whose nature is not to be docile, but rebellious, not weak, but strong. The "grace" we have discussed is the miracle that such a creature can become gentle toward us and love us. The one we love attracts and gives pleasure precisely because she possesses this force, which is free and liberating, but also unforeseeable and frightening. This is why in the succession of "proofs" that lead to love, the person who is more frightened imposes on the other a great many restrictions, a great many small sacrifices, all of which are basically intended to make her gentle, safe and innocuous. And the other person gradually accepts them. She has friends, but she decides not to go out with them; she used to travel, but now she stays home; she used to love her profession, but now she neglects it in order to devote herself to her lover. To avoid upsetting her lover, she imperceptibly eradicates everything that may have that effect. She makes many small renunciations, none of which is serious, none of which passes a point of no return. She gladly makes them, because she wants her lover to be happy; she tries to become what he wants her to be. Gradually, she becomes *domestic*, available, always ready, always grateful. In this way, the marvelous wild beast is reduced to a domestic pet; the tropical flower, plucked from its environment, droops in the little vase by the window. And the lover who asked her to become like this because he wanted to be reassured, because he was frightened by the new experience, winds up missing in her what he had previously sought and found. The person who stands before him is not the same one he had fallen in love with, precisely because at that time she was different and fully alive. He asked her to model herself on his fears, and now he faces the result of those fears—her nothingness—and he no longer loves her. This often happens with men who fall in love with a young girl, with her youth, her possibilities. But they are afraid of her, so they ask her to give up her job and friends, to stop being flirtatious and witty, until she becomes pliable and dull. At which point they realize that they desire another young girl, that they have destroyed the one they are now with. I haven't chosen this example by chance: it is women in particular who suffer this violence and adapt themselves to this role. They are desired as long as they are free, because they express the vitality of freedom; then they are confined to domestic life, to harems, surrounded by endless restrictions, by a jealousy that is only their lover's fear of wanting what he originally wanted; finally, they are forced to become an everyday banality, the place where by definition not only falling in love, but even love itself inevitably ends.

Yet the need to turn the other person into a banality, to remove his specificity and diversity, to tear away his vital forces, also exists in women. They learned it partly from men, over the centuries. Forced to become a domestic animal, a woman can do nothing to defend herself but impose the same fate on the man. Her profound insecurity makes her search for easy, manageable certainties, and there is nothing more easy or manageable than the person who has lost his vital energy, who acts out things that are repetitive and already familiar. Thus it often happens that both lovers, frightened by their desire to live intensely, slide rapidly toward boredom, bitterness and disappointment. They simply imagine that thousands of promises and restrictions will enable them to achieve the impossibility of living "happily ever after." Later they will be disappointed and disillusioned, and they will fantasize about the life they could have had but destroyed.

This is perhaps the most common way that falling in love gradually ends. But there are others. One derives from the fact that something that is beautiful in an extraordinary experience becomes unbearable in everyday life. Many people fall in love with someone who is esteemed by society, because he is a singer or pianist, a boxer or skier or writer. Let's take the case of the pianist. Here the extraordinary consists in musical success, in the world that surrounds this activity, the world of the performance, something that is socially extraordinary. Living with a pianist, however, is an entirely different story. And the same goes for all professions of this kind, because in reality they involve discipline, rehearsals, a constant drive toward a goal, an achievement, a perfection. The public sees none of this routine work, and neither does the person in love at the beginning. She is impressed by the performance and does not think of that humble, behind-the-scenes work that she will have to accept as necessary and learn to share in without being the protagonist. So it is very easy to be disappointed. But this chain of events also occurs with people who are not professionals. Some men, for example, are attracted to vivacious, enterprising women who are brilliant and active, but later these men feel they are being held back and dominated. Other men fall in love with maternal, solicitous women who care for them as if they were children. Later they feel controlled like children. Many women are attracted to gentle men who later prove to be weak; other women are attracted to rough men who prove to be brutish and obtuse. Excess, first seen as an extraordinary quality, can develop into another kind of excess later on.

Now let's look at another case, asking a question that many people ask. Is it true that we fall in love more easily with someone who resists and who thereby makes himself desirable? Is it true that if we have to choose between two people, we choose not the one who has fallen in love with us, but the one who avoids us? This is a very widespread idea which is partly true, but only to a small extent. Its truth lies in this: when we fall in love, we seek what is different and extraordinary. A person who is about to fall in love will find it very difficult to do so with someone who has loved her for a while and has been courting her; she already knows him and has already explored this alternative. Thus she cannot recognize the nascent state in him, cannot explore the possible in him, because he is already part of the past, of the familiar. She will be able to choose this solution only if she is disappointed in her search, only if someone else she loves fails to love her. Only then will she return to her past, taking refuge in the person who already loves her, certain of finding in him the availability and understanding that she has not found elsewhere. Yet she did not fall in love with the new person because he left, but only because he was new, different, unknown, open to possibility. Returning to the one who already loves her, she refuses to explore the possible and hence, in short, to fall in love. So she does not fall in love again. She may believe that she is in love, she may care deeply for him, she may have been living with him for much of her life, but here we are talking about love, not falling in love. Even if she convinces herself that she is in love, after a little while she will notice that she isn't any more. In reality, she finally learns what was true at the start—and what she had tried to ignore.

Let us go on to the final way that falling in love may end. This happens when someone has passed a point of no return, perhaps without even realizing it. No one knows where a point of no return lies. The only sign is an interior rebellion, a sense of desperation, the suspense—sometimes only for a few hours—that precedes apathy. But the point of no return may be concealed, put out of our mind in an impulse of generosity, or because the other person lets us know that one day things will change. Think of a woman who works and who loves her profession. The man she loves asks her to leave her work because his job requires him to move, and where he is going there will be no work for her. In a case like this, the woman may make the sacrifice, hoping that it will later be possible for her to resume her work. He may tell her that it is only for a little while, and then everything will change. It doesn't matter how; the fact remains that the point of no return has been passed. The woman leaves her job, her career, and follows her man; then she gradually notices that she no longer has any interests, that she no longer has any vitality, that again and again she longs for what she has left behind. She has fallen out of love.

At times, it is life, with its succession of events, that causes what has been set aside or postponed to reappear as a point of no return. A woman may have wanted a child profoundly, but in order not to destroy her love, she may have renounced this desire, postponing it to another time. But then things happen around her: her father dies, next her mother, she realizes that she is growing old, and suddenly, faced with the power of the negative, her capacity to create life takes on a new value. To have a child means to defeat death. What before was deferred now becomes urgent, an essential element of her plan. The pact—from which love arose—is discussed again or broken, and the dilemma explodes once more, but this time with no possibility of postponement. Her essential need demands to be understood and accepted. If it is not accepted, her love slowly fades as she now faces what seems to her an intolerable lack of understanding, an unjustified egotism. She begins to reexamine the past, calculating what she has given (so much) and what she has received (nothing). Love dies in resentment, and even the memory of it vanishes. Points of no return occur much more frequently in the course of life than we might imagine. Things that seemed secondary prove to be essential. In all these cases, everything appears as a way to put love slowly to sleep. In reality, however, if we look more carefully, we can perceive the reemergence of the dilemma and an undercurrent of desperation.

17

IS IT POSSIBLE FOR SOMEONE TO BE IN LOVE WITH AN-
other person for many years, or for his entire life? Yes. Is
it possible for two people to be in love for many years, or
for their entire lives? Yes. At first sight, it seems impossible, because falling in love is a transitional state that vanishes or is institutionalized or comes to an end. This is, in
fact, the normal range of possibilities. Yet there are exceptional cases in which the aim of the lover's plan is to
preserve the nascent state itself, in which one person continues to love the other passionately, even if the beloved is
inaccessible, or simply dead. Precisely because the beloved is no longer accessible—we think of Abélard's separation from Héloïse, the death of Dante's Beatrice, the
marriage and then death of Petrarch's Laura—and no rejection has occurred, the sense of falling in love can continue in the imagination. If there has been a rejection, it
will not continue; in this case, the conscience is forced to
fight against the past, "what was." But when the beloved
has said "yes," or just hasn't said "no," the entire creative
capacity of love can be directed toward her. And since
fantasy cannot be disproved by reality, this love can continue on the extraordinary level.

In order to understand what is involved here, we need

only think of those intervals in which the lovers are far away from one another, not because they have separated, but because of some external obstacle which they see as insuperable. Each of them lives in the other's heart, and their love becomes a constant longing for one another, a suffering, because they are not together, but also a constant source of the greatest joy in memories, in the wait or simply in thoughts of their love. Then everything that happens becomes incidental compared with this profound love that agitates and excites them. Life can unfold normally and even be active and generous, but its emotional and ethical center lies elsewhere. Love becomes the internal place of regeneration, an island withdrawn from the incidental, the rose garden in the middle of the desert, in which the soul quenches its thirst and from which it can return to the world. All of this is very close to mysticism. *The Divine Comedy* is in fact a great mystical poem, in which the beloved woman becomes a companion and guide on a mystical journey to God. In pure mysticism, this mediating figure disappears, and the love is addressed directly to God. But this mediating figure is not uncommon in real life. The relationship between Saint Clare and Saint Francis closely resembles an experience of falling in love transferred to (or sublimated in) divinity. Mawlana Jalal ud-din Rumi wrote the greatest mystical poem of Islam, the *Mathnawī*, as well as a collection of lyric poetry, the *Diwān*, after Shams-e Tabrizi, a man he deeply loved, had disappeared or died. In the *Mathnawī*, the poet never speaks of this man, only of God, but in many parts of the poem, the reader has the impression of a love so concrete and so consuming as to confuse the figures of the human Friend and the divine Friend. The *Diwān*, however, is explicitly dedicated to Shams-e Tabrizi, and here it is through the beloved Friend that the poet proceeds to speak of God.

Mystical love remains a nascent state because no mutual pact is possible with the divine Friend or Loved One. One can only love, the other can only be loved, and the latter's response, which cannot be guaranteed, is always "grace." Because of this total asymmetry, this unbridgeable distance, mystical love is always the revelation of being as love, and next to it everything else is incidental. Precisely because of this distance, what is striking in mystical love is the presence of a constant, incessant suffering that miraculously becomes joy. "My healing and my grief are both in you," Ramón Lull writes. "The more surely you heal me, the greater my grief grows: and the more I languish, the more you give me health."* Saint Teresa of Avila, even at the seventh level, the last and most perfect mystical state, finds that there "is a great desire to suffer, but this is not of such a kind as to disturb the soul, as it did previously. So extreme is her longing for the will of God to be done in her that whatever His Majesty does she considers to be for the best: if He wills that she should suffer, well and good; if not, she does not worry herself to death as she did before."†

---

* Lull, *The Book of the Lover and the Beloved*, p. 25.

† Saint Teresa of Avila, *Interior Castle*, trans. E. Allison Peers (New York: Doubleday and Company, 1961), p. 220.

Mysticism clearly shows us that falling in love does not depend in any way on the traits of the beloved: it is purely and simply our way of seeing (thinking, feeling, perceiving, imagining and so forth), a conceptual system that exists entirely in the structure of our mind. We do not see things as they are, but as we make them. Mystical love constructs its object on the basis of those features that distinguish the nascent state, and since this sort of love is unable to fasten on a living person (and transfigure him in the imagination), it constructs a pure, ideal object. Contemporary culture says that this is antithetical to life. It seems so to me too, but we must recognize that for millennia, mysticism has been a very important and intense way of life. In fact, the object does not cease to be real for the person who loves it. Yet in the normal experience of falling in love is the beloved any more "real"? The difference is that the normal experience is an imaginative creation that becomes a plan, that wants to modify reality in order to realize itself, to incarnate itself in the world. This is an impossible task, however, because there is always the incidental, the material, a collection of facts we must take into account. Every incarnation is a loss. As a result, every experience of falling in love that lasts a long time can only be created in the imagination, can only survive in the imagination, and asks the two lovers to renounce their desire to see, here and now, actually achieved, what they desire above every other thing. The more the experience of being in love insists on realizing everything in the concrete, in the pragmatic, in facts, the more it is doomed to extinction. In the end, we might just as well be coherent and say that we forgo the extraordinary experience, that we do not seek it, that we do not want it, or that we do not want it in that way. This applies not only to falling in love, but to every nascent state. The desire to have everything immediately in the concrete is the cause of the most terrible experiences of fanaticism. Life never incarnates the real completely. To claim that at a certain point we can realize an earthly paradise is fanaticism. Everything that exists can be transfigured, but it never becomes absolute, perfect, infallible, complete. There is always a point where reality intersects with passing facts, where the real shines through the incidental; it is the "self-revelation" of the absolute. The object of our love remains both empirical and transfigured. The mystic resolves the problem by annihilating the observable, by reducing it to pure accident, and he separates the real by making it an object of pure intuition. In other words, the mystic allows the mental work of the nascent state to construct its object.

At this point, however, we can see that one or both of the lovers may make important advances in this direction by not putting their love to the test of concrete, everyday incarnation. So the revolution fails, and the ideal is separated from existence, becoming the imaginary place where the encounter occurs. The lovers live their concrete lives, pass through the center of events in the world, struggle, construct things, but preserve the dimension of the extraordinary in their relationship. This happens infrequently, but it is not extremely rare. Nor is it easy to reveal, because these lovers do not talk about their love. Precisely because it is an imaginary space, they separate it completely from everyday life and are totally reticent and modest about it. It isn't necessary to imagine that this kind of love is purely spiritual or platonic. It may also be highly sexual. Why is it very rare? Obviously, because the experience of falling in love arises as the lover's plan to reconstruct his life concretely, to reorganize around a new person his entire present, past and future life, and to do it in a clear, exemplary way. It is a plan for concrete transformation, and therefore the kind of alternative we have been describing seems like failure to many people. Lovers adopt it only in certain circumstances, and generally after they have explored other paths that prove to be impractical. This is not to say that this kind of love lasts. The lovers' plan to realize their love in a total, concrete life together reemerges followed by another attempt, which often leads to the end of their love.

The curious relationship that can be constructed between the imaginary as real and the existing as incidental allows us to consider the different meanings that fantasy has in sexual relations. During sex many people fantasize that they are making love with another person, or with other different people, or with the same person but in a different situation. Even when someone falls in love, he may fantasize about his relationships with others. These fantasies, however, may ascribe to the loved one the valuable qualities of the lover's previous sexual partners. In the end, these partners disappear, and only the loved one remains. Sometimes, too, the lover may imagine the one he loves with someone else, or he may put himself in the place of someone with whom she was involved in the past.

In this case as well, the fantasies mean that the lover is ascribing to himself all those qualities to which he gives value. Jealousy also includes giving value, so that when the lover fantasizes that he is in the place of someone of whom he is jealous, he is annihilating that person as a value and replacing him completely. Yet the process is radically different for the lover who is having relations with others. While in the first case he empties his fantasies and assigns them to the beloved, in this case he does not assign them to his current sexual partner. In fact, with any partner he may have, he continues to imagine he is making love with the one he loves, and from those moments when he does not fantasize he extracts an experience that will later live again in his imagination when he is with his beloved. Thus we arrive at the paradox that a person may make love with someone he does not love without ever actually doing so, and he may never make love with someone he loves and yet do so only with her. There are in fact people who change their sexual partners constantly but continue to make love with the same person. And they may never mention it, not even in analysis or group therapy.

18

CAN THE EXPERIENCE OF FALLING IN LOVE BE TRANS-
formed into a love that preserves the freshness of that experience for years? Yes. This can happen when the two
lovers manage to lead a new, active, adventurous and interesting life together, in which they discover different
things or struggle against external difficulties together. Of
course, these difficulties cannot be too great, for when we
fall in love every external difficulty is reflected internally
as the idea that the lovers' plans are incompatible. But
there are some difficulties that are not consequences of the
lovers' past lives; in this case, they find themselves fight-
ing *side by side for a common plan.* This binds the two
plans together, minimizes the mutual tests because the
obstacle is experienced as external and not internal (rejection), and creates a solidarity in their shared action, in
which they want together what concerns each of them
individually and as a couple. Yet the extraordinary, adventurous element remains very important. The nascent
state is a revolution of everyday life, so it is able to develop when it has succeeded in revolutionizing the everyday, when life can take another direction that is new,
desired and interesting. In this case, the extraordinary en-
ergies of the nascent state give an immense strength to the

two lovers, so that they can confront the unknown and the different and overcome difficulties together.

When they begin a journey, an adventure or a new job in a faraway place, they feel they have strength and solidarity in themselves and only in themselves. This objective fact confirms what they have guessed: that their strength comes from their being together, from their love. But the different, the new, the extraordinary works in a very subtle way: it distances the everyday and reduces the weight of the past that always hangs over the creation of a plan. For this to happen, it is not necessary for the lovers to go to unknown places. They can remain in their native city, but they must have a reason to see it again in a completely different way; they must be able to construct new and significant itineraries for themselves. If they are forced to repeat steps they have already taken, to rediscover what they have already experienced, "what was" winds up crushing the possible. There is nothing that destroys the nascent state more completely than the repetition of sameness, having to relive experiences we have already had and finding all over again the same problems we were already familiar with and had already imagined or already experienced. Instead of a historicizing, a remaking of the past, what happens is that the past reappears and remakes the present and the future. But it is also true that what is new for one person may have already been experienced by another, may be a return of sameness for him. In this case, the lovers' plans become incompatible, and the experience of falling in love comes to an end.

What if there is no active, different life? In this case, the only alternative is the interior journey, the mystical voyage we discussed in the preceding chapter. But this is so rare. In reality, everyone looks for the active, external journey, the active life, because this is what satisfies the burning need to transform life as the nascent state would have it. To try new things together: this is the key to prolonging the state of falling in love. These new shared experiences can be like a "vacation," an interruption of the everyday. But, in general, a vacation is not enough, because the everyday winds up imposing itself on these brief interruptions, which appear as escapes, as adventures in the world of the imagination. The greatest break comes when the new shared experiences really cut into the routine of everyday life and suggest a real alternative or when, while still only a "vacation," they allow for a discovery, a search, a seeing with new eyes as a couple, a deciphering of a different reality, and become so significant as to leave a lasting impression. The honeymoon is one way in which the old institutions tried to deal with this need, channeled it, offered it a ready-made response. The honeymoon is the institutional symbol of this vacation from the everyday, this adventure of a profoundly shared life. The trip that is often recommended to two spouses who are "tired of each other" is also an attempt to revitalize, through an extraordinary event, the experience of the extraordinary which has now been choked and stifled by the banality of everyday routines and by the accumulation of disappointments.

What in fact is the banality of the everyday, if not the failure of the transforming and revolutionizing processes that the nascent state initiated? Falling in love is an exploration of the possible; the person we fall in love with offers us a way to modify our everyday experience radically. And the beloved, too, when she falls in love, becomes more vivacious, more fanciful, more capable of making plans; she lets us glimpse a richer, more diverting, more fascinating life composed of intense emotions, marvelous things, continual discoveries, even risks. The everyday gradually comes to stand as a rejection of all this. The turning point, of course, occurs with the great sacrifices, the points of no return, but the change happens gradually, as the lovers make little compromises, follow customary routines, and give into laziness, convenience, lack of imagination or fear of taking risks. Even at the beginning, when a great upheaval has occurred, when the two lovers decide to live together, divorce their spouses or change their jobs, they collide with the countless known and recurring facts of everyday life, the countless obligations that subordinate their imaginations to the everyday until it imposes its dictatorship once more. We try to subvert this dictatorship with vacations, parties, psychotherapy, different sexual encounters. But there is nothing in everyday life that can transcend its banality except an affirmation of the superiority of the imagination over reality, its constant struggle against existence—which is to say another nascent state. Hence even a great transformation often falls headlong into a new version of the everyday, into another inextricable net of obligations. The nascent state, by becoming love and reconstructing a new order, has carried out its transformative task: another job, another house, other friends and children remain. Anyone who divorces and remarries one, two, three times often rediscovers a situation that is not very different from the initial one. Of course, this all happens to him and the other person without their knowing beforehand; but it shows that they cannot will the world to become luminous and always reborn.

So the experience of falling in love disappears and love takes its place. For it to continue, however, as we saw at the beginning of this chapter, the extraordinary experience must somehow continue in everyday life, must be realized as an extraordinary journey through existence which the lovers make together, side by side, after difficult tests, after discovery and confrontation, after constant reinterpretation of the world and constant reexamination of the past. For some, this may be a struggle, a kind of poetry; for others, simply the capacity to be constantly amazed by themselves and the world, as they constantly seek not what is reassuring or what has already been noted, but what is challenging, beautiful, creative. In this sense, the external journey is only the occasion, the vehicle for a continuous internal journey, just as the internal journey is continuously the stimulus for an external journey. In these situations, the experience of falling in love continues because the nascent state is reborn over and over, in a constant revision, rediscovery, renewal, self-renewal, a constant search for challenges and opportunities. Then we fall in love again with the same person. This requires the initiative to come from both lovers. If one of them is passive, if he waits for the other to make plans, or does not have the courage to propose them, or simply does not know how to profit from his opportunities and looks for *the* opportunity, any transformation rapidly falls under the dictatorship of the everyday and leads to resentment. Yet if one of the lovers, no matter how creative he may be, makes choices that rigorously limit their experience to habitual channels—a certain kind of job that absorbs him, having children, sick parents that must be cared for constantly and so forth—the other lover's constant attempts to discover the new all fail and provoke frustration in her. In the end, two different kinds of plans clash, and the ordinary plan always prevails over the extraordinary one.

I don't think there is any practical rule for how to behave—an art of staying in love—to be drawn from all this. Such rules are always instruments of self-deception, of falsification. Life creates the nascent state, it creates the encounter, the plans, the tests and the opportunities, and it takes them away. We are afloat in this great sea like a small canoe in the middle of a storm. We don't make the waves, nor do we modify them. We can stay afloat, happily or with difficulty or in both ways, we may reach the shore or not reach it, and find joy in arriving or in not arriving. Perhaps more than an art of loving or of falling in love, we need to know what we are really dealing with in order to make our decisions, always keeping in mind our humanity.

19

THIS IS A BOOK ABOUT FALLING IN LOVE, NOT ABOUT love itself. But in order to understand falling in love fully, we need to say something about love as well, that more stable and lasting bond toward which falling in love tends, insofar as it has a goal. The nascent state tends in fact to become an institution, and the institution consists fundamentally in this: in saying, in maintaining that *on the symbolic level the nascent state is fully realized and at the same time is yet to be realized in practice.* In the October Revolution, total liberation, the classless society and equality among human beings were symbolically established, so much so that the plenum of the central committee must make decisions unanimously, and elections are held to show that there is no dissent. At the same time, however, what is realized is not communism, but the dictatorship of the proletariat, a stage on the way to communism, which is yet to be realized. The institution, by separating the symbolic level from the practical, defines itself as the harbinger of a real event. The elements of the nascent state lie at the heart of institutions, but its actual appearance—having been symbolically realized—is postponed to an increasingly distant future, like Judgment Day in Christianity. Yet since the nascent state is declared to be realized on the symbolic level, our symbols and rituals claim to reactivate it, to make it live again. The liturgical year is nothing other than this very symbolic evocation of the divine time of origins and its sacred events, in which men are invited to participate. But institutions consist not only in rituals; they are in the souls of men and women. To a certain extent, then, they effectively reactivate the original values; they stamp our time with these meanings and these values. What we have called everyday life is therefore rich in moments when something is revealed or reappears—not like the eternal return of what is already well known, but like the rediscovery of what is. To establish a link between falling in love and these ideas without writing another book, I will take a shortcut and discuss an experience I have already mentioned, the gift. For the sake of simplicity, I will limit myself to four examples.

When do we say that a relationship is not authentic? When we view the other person as a means to obtain a result, to get something; when she (or he) comes between us and the things we desire and we must work on her to get them; when she has power over us and we must influence her by begging or flattery. We would like to do without her; at every moment, we would rather not have to depend on her. And when we can do without her, when we no longer need her, we forget about her; she ceases to exist for us. Many of our relationships in work are of this type, if not nearly all of them. Here gifts and good wishes are, fundamentally, hypocritical and servile. They are hypocritical because they try to say, "This gift means that I value you, that I care about you," while in reality we think, "I need him; I must ingratiate myself with him." They are servile because the gift is the recognition that the other person has power over us, however limited it may be. Gifts move upward, toward the powerful: whoever receives the most good wishes or the most gifts is the most powerful. These things are a sort of tithe that the weak impose on themselves for the powerful. The mass of postcards, letters, telegrams and packages is the visible evidence of the geography of power in society. If power shifts, everything else shifts too.

Next year many people will not receive gifts. Their power will have passed; they will have been forgotten. But even today the gift signifies: "I would like to be able to forget about you, to ignore you, to remove you from my life, but I can't; in fact, I must do the complete opposite. . . . One day, however, I won't need you any more, and I'll drive you back into the nothingness that you never should have left." This is one source of inauthenticity on holidays. They should be one thing, but they become something else; they should be a time of love, but they become the celebration of servile homage. And this creates uneasiness, discomfort, the impression of insincerity. These feelings mean that holidays are also a time of servility; otherwise we would not feel uncomfortable. If holidays seem inauthentic to us, it means that we profoundly know what is authentic or what should be.

But there is another class of gifts. These are the ones we give to people who are really close to us, whom we know are close: our parents, our children, our husband or wife, our brothers and sisters, a few friends, sometimes even the few who have power over us but whom we love and want to be with. A gift presented to those we love is not a servile homage: it is testimony to a relationship that will not be broken. In this case, the gift really says: "I love you, I continue to love you, even if it doesn't seem so, even if I don't see you as often as I should. I haven't forgotten you." Because in reality we do forget. We forget for months, for years. We forget our parents, our husband or wife, our children. Above all, we forget people who are far away, but sometimes even those who are nearby. We really don't have a constant relationship with the people we love. We encounter them at certain points, every so often, as we do with a friend who lives far away. And when they are near, when they live with us, they command our attention simply because they are there. We don't feel a constant need for them; we act because we must, out of habit, as a duty, sometimes complaining. And yet we are tied to them, and we realize it if we should lose them or if we run the risk of losing them—when they are sick, when they do not come home, when they might die. Then anguish assails us, and we discover that they are essential. Then we discover that they have a very high value, next to which everything else loses its importance and becomes incidental. Yet their value, the fact that they are essential, becomes clear to us only when we may lose them, as the fear of losing them. In those moments, the world is divided in two: they are on one side, while on the other is *the power of the negative* that may take them away from us. To the kidnapper, illness, death, they have no value. The power of these things consists only in depriving us of certain people: it is nonbeing as power. On holidays we recognize these people; the gift is a testimony to the fact that they are essential for us. We cannot give them just any gift: we must choose one that is appropriate to them, something that really gives them pleasure, something that speaks to their profound individuality, to the essential nucleus of their person, something that *enriches their vital essence.* At these times, we give gifts in order to nourish them, to strengthen them, to make their lives strong and happy against the shadow of nonbeing—not only sickness and death, but also indifference and forgetfulness, including our own.

Then there is a third class of gifts, the gifts of loving, of being in love and falling in love.

How do we know when we are in love? Because we fall in love again, because we repeatedly fall in love with the same person. When we are in love, there are times when we have the impression that the other person doesn't matter at all. We want to do without her (or him); we part and tell ourselves: "It was an infatuation; now it's over; she doesn't matter to me. I'm free." Sometimes we run into her, and she says nothing to us; she is indifferent, and we angrily ask ourselves what we saw in her. Then it happens again. That indifferent face, that voice become unique; her absence becomes unbearable, her presence infinite joy. Everything about her moves us; everything about her brings nostalgia and satisfaction. This is extraordinary eros: this is the will that finds its object. We look at her and we can't believe that she is there, for us, because we can't believe that we have everything we desire—the fullness of life that says "yes" to us. At this point, the negative and its power no longer exist: the loved one fills our consciousness and makes us happy. Then, after hours or days, she vanishes once again, as if she had been an illusion, and our everyday ego, our everyday world, returns. Are we really in love? But the extraordinary reappears. It always reappears new and different; like a unique object of desire, it impresses itself on us. And it impresses itself on us again and again until everything else disappears. Being prevails over the everyday world, degrades it; love is nothing other than this dominance. What becomes of the gift in this case?

We would like to give everything, but it never seems enough to us because we want to give the best part of ourselves, what has the most value in us, in the hope that it may be the same for her, that it will be welcomed. We give in the hope of appearing to her just as she appears to us, in the hope of being welcomed into her and of finding peace. The gift is a way to join symbolically with being in its dominance, its manifestation, its birth.

I have spoken about falling in love in a strict sense, but perhaps love, particularly the strongest love, presents itself to us in the same way: as falling in love, as falling in love again and again with the same person. A parent's love for his child takes this form too. For the mother, the child is there; he is present because he cries, because he needs something, because he may be in danger, because he is frustrated. But every so often during the day or at night, or when she is far away or when she looks at him, he "appears" to her as an object that evokes desire, nostalgia, infinite tenderness, total self-fulfillment. The mother constantly falls in love with her child. And not only when he is young, but also when he is grown, when he is an adult. Every so often, she sees him, she looks at him with astonished, passionate eyes, recognizing the fact that he is with her. The lover thanks the beloved for existing. This is not a question of seeing in the adult the child who is no longer there. No, she sees the adult just as she used to see the child; she looks at him and falls in love with what he is today. Every time she rediscovers the completeness of what he is. It is a rebirth of passion; it is always "the first day." Everyone, even the poorest person, has been given this gift, which lays the foundation for the value of existence, an absolute foundation in something that has value in itself and is rediscovered. Those who lose the hope of rediscovering it die.

But perhaps—I say "perhaps" because not every child psychologist would agree—childhood is completely based on this experience. The child makes demands, is thwarted, makes himself autonomous. But at any moment he may want to be held, caressed, hugged; at night, he wants someone next to him while he goes to sleep; a kiss makes him happy and greedy for more. Perhaps he falls in love each time, perhaps each time—a dizzying number of times—he has the astonishing, incredible experience of the fullness of life that says "yes." He detaches himself from it in order to become autonomous, yet he rediscovers it every time, he comes upon the revelation and reconfirms it every time. With this cement, he builds the trust to be here, the ability to live in the world.

In this last case—a parent's love for his child—the gift has two aspects: from one point of view, it appears as a gift of the self; but from another point of view, it is a gift that gives consistency to the child's life. But the child also gives gifts. I don't mean the flowers he brings to his mother, but his words, the astonishing linguistic constructions that mature within him and that he utters at a certain point. With his words, he builds a door, a house, a castle into which the adult can enter because it is a house for him. It is also a house the adult can complete with the child, in a shared activity. The child's words are the first song of a completely objectified love, like truly great poetry, but at the same time, they are also an activity that he does side by side with his parents.

In this survey, the reader will also have found a place for other important things in life. But he will have seen that the experience of falling in love has its own peculiar place with respect to everything that exists in time and that reaffirms itself and recurs.

20

THIS BOOK IS CERTAINLY BOUND TO DISPLEASE THREE groups of people: those who move in a utilitarian, pragmatic orbit; those who adhere to ideological systems like Catholicism, Islam and Marxism; and, lastly, those who are currently engaged in a critique of the heterosexual couple—many feminists, for example.

For the utilitarians, the entire discourse is finally nonsense, because it rests on the assumption that there is a social condition—the nascent state and hence also the institution that follows it to some extent—in which a metaphysical distinction is maintained between the real and the ephemeral. This is a distinction that constantly reappears in philosophy: it is drawn between idea and appearance (Plato), form and matter (Aristotle), essence and accident (Saint Thomas Aquinas), reason and intellect (Hegel), the class for itself and the class in itself (Marx), the will to power and the reactive force (Nietzsche), and so on. This distinction is foreign to utilitarian thought. Let us take as an example of utilitarianism its most typical product: economics. The science of economics is possible only if things can be compared and exchanged; it has nothing to do with absolute values, only with interests. A good deal of sociology and psychology are utilitarian in origin insofar as they do not have any means of dealing with absolute value and consequently wind up denying its specificity, its spontaneity, or even its existence. Yet this way of thinking is not limited to the social sciences. In our everyday life, we reason in terms of utility, interests, means, advantages and disadvantages. In fact, we can say that utilitarianism is the way of thinking in everyday life. We have already said that the everyday considers enthusiasm, disinterestedness and passion as forms of irrationality; it protects itself from them and does not want to be upset by them. All this is logical and comprehensible, but if we want to comprehend falling in love, we must keep in mind that it contradicts this way of thinking. As a result, it cannot be explained by utilitarianism.

The issue becomes more complex when we move on to Christianity, Islam and Marxism. In technical terms, these are *cultural civilizations.* They too are institutional powers springing from a movement (the original forms of Christianity or Islam) that produced a kind of institution whose distinctive trait is the absorption of other movements, giving them its language and symbols. During medieval Christianity, for example, every possible revolt, every possible religious experience, every cultural movement wound up defining itself in Christian terms. Every movement, in order to speak and make itself understood, was forced to take as a fixed point the fundamental nucleus of Christianity: the passion and death of Jesus Christ, the sacraments, the priesthood, orthodoxy and heterodoxy, and so on. A cultural civilization, in other words, offers models with which both ordinary and extraordinary experiences must be interpreted; everything else is *deprived of language*. What we have said about Christianity applies to Islam as well. In the area where this civilization has spread, every movement uses the language of Islam.

A civilization also imposes its language and its institutions on the nascent state that characterizes the experience of two people falling in love. In Christian marriage, for example, there is no distinction among falling in love, love, devotion and sexuality. The sacrament of matrimony implies all these things at once. What it tends to affirm is devotion (the relationship) and sexuality (reproduction); everything else has no particular value. This imposition has prevailed even in our time. In several European languages, including French and English, there is no word for falling in love as there is an Italian (*innamoramento*). The word "fall" (*tomber*) is used. In Provençal, a word existed (*adamare*), but it was repressed with the Catharist heresy.* Christianity draws a distinction between love for men and love for God (adoration). In the eyes of a church father, falling in love, as we have described it, would seem a painful aberration or simply an

* The Catharist heresy is associated with a widespread ascetic sect that flourished during the Middle Ages and was finally suppressed by the Catholic Church in the fourteenth century. It asserted the Manichaean doctrine that the universe is composed of two mutually opposed principles—one good, the other evil—and rejected certain orthodox beliefs and institutions, including the divine authorship of the Old Testament and marriage. De Rougement has argued a connection between this heresy and Provençal love poetry (*Love in the Western World*, pp. 74–101). [Translator's note.]

instance of idolatry. There are other examples of this distinction: "grace" for Christianity is a divine intervention; in our analysis, it is a human experience. For the Christian, all the theological terms we have borrowed would be improper or merely metaphors. My point is that they comprise the language which the Christian cultural civilization has given to the nascent state. As far as falling in love is concerned, it is often the only language we possess.

The case of Marxism is in many respects identical to that of Catholicism and Islam. Marxism also springs from a movement and grows by absorbing other movements. At its center lies the experience of the nascent state (the end of alienation, communism, prehistory-history and so on). It too lends its language to every revolutionary movement, and those that do not adopt this language remain inarticulate. For Marxists, however, the subject (the "we") is the class. And the class undergoes a transubstantiation (the nascent state, in our term) in the shift from the class *in itself* to the class *for itself*. For Marxism, then, no collective movement is possible unless it involves a class, and when there is a collective movement that either does not involve a class or does not define itself in class terms, Marxism denies its existence or importance and refuses to consider it in the same category as the class movement.

From the Marxist point of view, religious movements constitute the first, rudimentary consciousness of a condition of exploitation and alienation, but as long as this does not embrace a consciousness of class and proletarian internationalism, it remains false consciousness, prehistory. The experience of falling in love, then, which has nothing to do with class and which even unites people who are members of two different classes, belongs to the private, the irrational, to what has no science and should not have one. Since falling in love has the properties of a movement but cannot be reduced to a class, it appears to be bourgeois or merely reactionary. This is not to say that Marx, Lenin and Mao Zedong were not in love; they fell in love just as other people do. But this dimension of their lives was cut off from the public one; it was considered private, devoid of value, at the most a subject of gossip.

Now let us consider feminism. This too is a movement, and like every Western movement, it is based on the characteristic experiences of the nascent state (the separation of the essential from the inessential, authenticity, self-awareness, historicization—in other words, mythic time, prehistory, the arrival of feminism, the final liberation of woman—communism, equality and so forth). The dividing line here, however, is drawn between men and women. The "we" of feminism is constituted by women, not men. Like every movement, feminism also separates people who were united and unites those who were separated: it unites women and separates them from men. In contrast, bisexual love separates a man and a woman from something else (the family, kinship, class and so on) and unites them. The feminist movement, then—above all, in its nascent state—can only consider falling in love absurd and senseless. But how can it consider as an object of absolute value an experience that makes woman a slave, that belongs to her historical oppressors, that shares their way of thinking and feeling, their gestures, all their properties?

Feminism has split the couple to create feminist solidarity and has attacked—"demystified"—falling in love because in modern society it is through this experience and its language that the couple is constituted and legitimized. But feminism has not had a program of persecution, has not transformed the male into something to be destroyed or suppressed, as Marxism, for example, has declared that it wants to do with the bourgeoisie. Feminism is an ethical movement that wants to transform the world by convincing individuals, not by destroying them. So it has wound up salvaging many aspects of falling in love in order to study them. Yet precisely by reinserting a distance between men and women and making women more autonomous, more aware, stronger, feminism has re-created the conditions of that tension between different things which constitutes the essence of falling in love. As feminism has matured, furthermore, women have learned to protect themselves from the moral enslavement that can occur in love, to want a real equality rather than a melodramatic declaration of it, to attach less importance to things like virginity, and to strip the rhetoric of falling in love of many of its falsehoods. Perhaps the very maturation of feminism constitutes the cultural precondition that will permit a thorough examination of love and remove it from the sphere of the sublime and from scorn.

Let's look at these things from another point of view. Utilitarianism, Christianity and Marxism are three real historical forces that operate in our society by acting as conceptual systems through which the world is seen and interpreted. Each of them, to use one of Foucault's terms, constitutes an *episteme*, a collection of rules imposed on a given historical period, the only ones that allow us to think and, above all, to speak about something.* Only by making his own discourse conform to the structures of discursive practice, Foucault observes, can the subject enter discourse, seize the word. The only "serious" discourse in any epoch is that of the dominant episteme. In our epoch, then, a knowledge of falling in love is produced only in the utilitarian system, or in Christianity or Marxism. What happens is that all three reduce falling in love to something else. Hence we do not have a true and proper scientific, religious or ideological way to understand it. On these levels, it does not exist, cannot be spoken. What language, then, is assigned to love? The language of great poetry or minor literature, the language of love letters, memoirs, comic strips. Silent on the scientific, religious and ideological levels, the nascent state of falling in love has only two linguistic alternatives at its disposal: it may choose the language of the sublime, the ineffable or, with an immense leap, that vulgar, popular language in which it is subject to ridicule and scorn.

This impossibility of finding a suitable language affects not only educated people; it is a fact that influences everyone's life. Lacking a language, no one has the means to think and reflect on what he experiences, to speak about it and communicate it to others. Confined to the ineffable or the contemptible, the person in love feels himself a

* Michel Foucault, *The Order of Things*, trans. A. M. Sheridan Smith (New York: Pantheon Books, 1971).

stranger in the concrete culture where he lives; he has the impression that his experience is totally personal and not collective. Since he must utilize definitions, formulas and explanations that are always distorting or inadequate, that always serve another end (ideological, political or religious), the more he wants to clarify his thoughts and feelings, the more he creates confusion; the more he tries to solve his problems, the more he complicates them; and the more he seeks advice from experts, the more he is confused. If we rely on a hackneyed but still frequently used expression, we can say that the official culture, whether political, scientific or religious, "represses" the nascent state involving two people, making it something that we cannot talk about in an appropriate way. From this point of view, even psychoanalysis, in all its forms, involves a denial because it attaches importance to sexuality and reduces all experience to sexual transformations. In the nineteenth century, the process of denial was inverted; then the language of romantic love served as the means to deny sexuality. Today the contrary happens: sexuality, talk about sexuality and sexual practices serve to repress, to render unconscious other desires, other forms in which eros manifests itself. Conformity and denial still exist as they have before; they have only changed their appearance.

21

IS FALLING IN LOVE ANTISOCIAL BEHAVIOR? ISN'T IT AN escape into privacy, an evasion of public and political obligations? This attitude is typical of the repressive culture we have mentioned. It is widespread and often repeated, but it does not have the slightest scientific foundation, the slightest evidence in its favor. In every great political movement, we find people in love among leaders as well as followers. In the great collective eruption of national liberation during the last century in Europe, the term "romantic" served to indicate a political orientation, a literary orientation and a distinctive experience of falling in love. But even after this period, we continue to find couples who participated in a collective movement while they were in love. In the Mazzinian, anarchic sphere, for example, it is enough to think of Anita and Giuseppe Garibaldi.* In the Marxist movement, the exact same thing has happened.

---

* A reference to Giuseppe Mazzini (1805–1872), a political thinker, writer and insurrectionist who advocated the overthrow of absolute rule in Italy and the formation of a republic. "Anita" was Anna Maria Ribiero da Silva, a Brazilian woman with whom the Italian patriot Garibaldi eloped during an exile in South America (1836–48). His companion on several military campaigns, she died in 1849 while they were trying to escape the Austrian army. [Translator's note.]

These facts alone show that the concept of an egotistic love that makes political involvement impossible is a falsification. Yet precisely when we spoke of the ways that falling in love can be prolonged (or that love can preserve the freshness of this experience), we said that the ideal condition is the active, adventurous life, the side-by-side struggle. With the conceptual instruments we have at our disposal, we can now examine this point more thoroughly.

Like every other movement, falling in love springs, at the individual level, from an excess of depression. This depression is due to the increase of ambivalence toward an object, individual or collective, which was first accepted and loved, but which gradually turns out to be disappointing, unfair and incompatible with the development of historical and vital forces (in Marxist terms, the productive forces). In such a situation, individuals explore alternatives. These are not only individual alternatives (another person), but essentially collective, ideal alternatives (another way of life). What I have described as the preparation for falling in love is a preparation for a different way of seeing, feeling, thinking, acting, being together. At this point, the person who seeks a more intense life, a true solidarity, may encounter someone else who is in the same situation, and then both of them experience the nascent state of falling in love. Yet if the historical structural conditions are suitable, if there are general conditions of ethnic, religious, national or class conflict, if the need for a new solidarity and a new justice has spread through thousands of people, then a nascent state involving an entire group occurs, there is a political, religious or class collective movement, and the individual finds recognition in this. Of course, if there are no historical conditions suited to a collective movement, all this does not happen. But if individual historical conditions conducive to falling in love are lacking, this does not happen either. Thus there are certain preconditions for falling in love and others for collective processes. When these two sets of preconditions coexist, the individual falls in love, the other person falls in love with him, and together they enter the movement and constitute an elementary cell within it. It's very possible for a couple in love to enter a movement: they enter it as a unit.

But there is more. Since the features of the nascent state (the real-the incidental, authenticity, equality, prehistory-arrival, communism, essential needs and so forth) are in large part the same whether it involves two people or a group, it is very easy to recognize the smaller movement in the larger one. In other words, the enamored couple "recognizes itself" in the movement and tends to blend with it. At this point, a problem of *exclusivity* may arise. The nascent state involving two people in fact leads to the formation of a couple who participate passionately in the movement but who, notwithstanding this participation, remain erotically sealed off. They go in search of friendship, solidarity, a general purpose, but they do not admit other lovers to their internal circle. By the same token, the collective movement leads to the formation of a group that tends to become exclusive. In this process, it can undergo an ideological evolution in which "communism" is extended to the sexes. This is an idea that can even originate in the couple itself, who may feel the desire to let other people participate in their happiness or, more simply, may not want to make anyone suffer. We have an example of this situation in Nikolai Chernyshevsky's book *What Is to Be Done?* However things turn out, the two alternative projects collide at a certain point, and the conflict presents itself as a dilemma on this occasion too. The evolution of the process depends on where the points of no return are situated. In some groups, the exclusive love of the couple is considered an obstacle to the full development of total communism. In other collective movements, however, it is welcomed as a point of no return and accepted as the individuals' right. During the Protestant Reformation, for example, the love between two people was accepted in Lutheranism and Calvinism. But with the Anabaptists at Münster, community among the sexes was imposed. In most of the anarchic communes in Italy and Andalusia, the couple was accepted, but in certain Russian nihilist groups, it was not.

But doesn't the fact that we frequently tend to fall in love with people of the same religion or the same ideology (with brethren, patriots, comrades) mean that we fall in love with those who are very similar to us, who share our ideas and ideals? And doesn't this contradict what we said earlier—namely, that falling in love always requires a difference, a transgression? To give a precise answer to these questions, it is necessary to distinguish clearly between two cases: that in which brethren, comrades and friends are formed in a movement and that in which these terms indicate membership in a church, a party or an associa-

tion. Before a movement arises, there are no brethren, patriots or comrades. They are the product of the movement's fusion. People who were previously separated,
who thought differently, who had different experiences
"recognize" each other in the nascent state of the movement and discover a solidarity which they did not feel before. This bears repetition: before the movement, this
solidarity, this enthusiasm, this community of ideas did
not exist at all. Although the people in question had certain conditions in common, they were different and separate. The process of fusion occurs in the movement, and
the result of this process—not its cause—is the fact that
these people share the same values, the same ideals and
the same project. What produces the recognition is not a
preexisting resemblance, but the resemblance engendered
by the nascent state. Consider, for example, the recent Islamic movement in Iran which overthrew the Shah in the
course of a few months. There had been numerous opposition groups in the past—liberals, Marxists, terrorists,
Muslims. It was only in the movement that they found a
common solidarity and a common goal. At that moment,
they minimized what divided them; they did not assign
any importance to past differences; they had common
ideals, and they felt that they had always had them. In reality, the movement produced them. There were differences, then, that were eliminated or reduced by the
movement. Thus, within the nascent state of the movement, people generally do not fall in love because differences are annihilated by the group. Yet what happens in
everyday life? We are more likely to fall in love

when we are members of a party or a church than when we are not. The reason for this, of course, is that such institutions offer greater opportunity to be with other people, to create relationships, to be recognized. The same thing can be said of a business, a sports team, a neighborhood. In all these cases, having common interests and common values is a facilitating factor. When we go beyond certain differences, we cannot fall in love. At the same time, however, we cannot fall in love with someone whom we don't know, who doesn't speak to us.

Here, then, are our conclusions. If two people in search of a different kind of solidarity meet each other while a great collective movement is about to erupt, they will fall in love, and their love will be channeled into the movement, recognizing itself in the latter's ideology and values. In this case, the couple enter the movement as a unit. The nascent state of the movement does not touch them. As a result, falling in love is more frequent at the beginning of great movements and often precedes them. When two people enter the movement separately, however, they tend to identify with the group or the leader, and they do not fall in love exclusively with each other. Being in love regains its importance when the movement enters a period of decline, when the nascent state survives in the participants' hearts as nostalgia, as a profound, consuming desire for an ideal world that can no longer be found in collective action. In this case, what is lost at the collective level can be rediscovered, with all its political, religious or ideological values, when two people fall in love. The two lovers then feel that they are the tiny nucleus of a greater movement. To use an expression from a song by Ivan Della Mea, "You and I form an alliance."* Here the alliance is socialist; falling in love is experienced as a unit within a greater movement, the socialist movement.

What, then, is the source of the widespread idea that falling in love is an egotistic, enclosed experience?

Its source is the political, religious or ideological institution that claims to have control over individuals.

Many groups, many institutions born of movements, require that the individual be totally dedicated to the group. Consider, for example, the Catholic monastic orders. In the beginning, many of these arose from movements that were made up of both men and women. Later, however, when an order was created, when the institution appeared, men were separated from women, and a rule of absolute obedience to superiors was put into practice. The same thing happens in political or revolutionary groups where an iron discipline is established. For these exclusive groups who want absolute dedication and complete obedience from the individual, the couple constitutes an obstacle, a restriction, a deprivation of the total power of the group. In other words, the *totalitarian group* feels that it is *de-prived* by the resistance of individuals who preserve an area inaccessible to its power. This area, withdrawn from the totalitarian power of the group, is called *private*. From the group's point of view, that restriction, that de-

---

* Born in Lucca in 1940, Ivan Della Mea is a popular songwriter and singer who began recording in the 1960s. His songs treat Italian social and cultural issues from a Marxist perspective. [Translator's note.]

privation, that "private" area is a limitation, a loss. So the group combats it and declares it egotistic, worthless. This is the source of the negative judgment that Marxist groups in particular give to the experience of falling in love. Such a judgment is an ideological operation, completed when this private area (as a de-privation of the group) is associated with "private property," property withdrawn from the political monopoly of the state or the party. These two phenomena are obviously not the same thing, but since both involve a subtraction from a monopolistic claim to power, they are ideologically assimilated. The more totalitarian the ideological, religious or political system, the more hostility is manifested toward whoever wants to withdraw himself from its power. In this sense, the system is also hostile toward the couple in love, since two lovers form the smallest social unit capable of defying it.

22

IS IT POSSIBLE TO FALL OUT OF LOVE BY CHOICE? NO. IS IT possible to avoid falling in love by choice? Yes. What can the will do while we are in the process of falling in love? It can decide to break off the relationship, not to see the other person any more, to leave her (or him). These are all actions that the will can perform. And as long as the beloved is present, nothing seems easier to do. Being in love gives us an extraordinary strength that allows us to say "no." But this strength instantly disappears when we have performed the irreparable act by which we lose our love, and then apathy and nostalgia appear.

Yet there is a kind of wisdom aimed at avoiding love. It is disseminated in all institutions, because they all face the problem of frustrating love or containing its effects—at least on certain levels. Since all institutions spring from and are revitalized through collective movements, they always have at their center something that they hold more important than any individual. This thing—which may be a party, movement, class, nation, church or God—is by definition superior to any concrete man or woman. The institution possesses a kind of wisdom that devalues the deification of any person, and anyone who belongs to an institution acquires this wisdom. For two thousand years, the Catholic Church has educated its priests to prefer heavenly sentiments to earthly ones by avoiding temptations and by confessing even sins of desire, and has intervened at the right time with its authority. To avoid love, Stendhal wrote, it is necessary to act immediately, in the very first moments; if we delay, we may be too late.* Anyone who does not want to fall in love must immediately shatter the first nucleus of attraction: if he likes someone, he must go with someone else; if he finds himself looking at a house two times in a row, he must move to another city; if he notices that he takes pleasure in being admired, he must do something to provoke scorn. A manual for avoiding love would very closely resemble a guide to the ascetic life, in which even sexuality is utilized to escape "the fall."

But why so much effort? What remains so attractive about falling in love that, despite all its problems, it constitutes such a great temptation? All we have said gives us an answer to this question. What constitutes the temptation in the Western world is not falling in love, but the nascent state. We are attracted by falling in love because we have learned to be attracted by the nascent state. This learning process occurs precisely in those institutions that—as we have seen—represent this state as symbolically realized but as still to be realized in practice. The principal institutions of the West, religious as well as political, ancient as well as modern, are all founded on the

* Stendhal, *Love*, trans. Gilbert and Suzanne Sale (New York: Farrar, Straus, 1957).

categories of the nascent state. We are attracted by the nascent state because it is the dream of the West. The ancient pre-Christian mysteries related the death and rebirth of a god, just as the essential feast days of Christianity are the Nativity—Christmas—and the Resurrection—Easter. At the end of time, Christianity promises the resurrection of the body and the New Jerusalem. Islam, which is completely Western in this sense, teaches that we must wait for Judgment Day. Marxism speaks of revolution, of renewal, of the end of history. To indicate a positive historical period, we use expressions like "renaissance," "risorgimento," "reconstruction," "renewal." In the darkness of the present, we await a new day, a new life, a new spring, a redemption, a ransoming, a liberation, a revolt. What attracts us is always the divine time of origins, situated in the past (as with religious myths), in the future (as with Marxism) or in the present (as with the experience of falling in love). This is the cultural tradition of the West.

Yet what is the ultimate dream for the West is a nightmare to be avoided for the East, particularly for the Hindu and Buddhist cultures. "Birth is pain; sickness, old age, death are pain; being tied to someone who does not love us is pain; being separated from someone who loves us is pain." So speaks Siddhartha Gautama, the enlightened one, the Buddha, interpreting an idea that is already present in the Hindu texts. To be reborn means to return to the hell of life, inevitably to encounter pain. The nascent state, from this point of view, is the greatest of illusions. We cannot enter the Garden of Eden and remain there: we can enter it only to be driven out continually, perpetually. We face a constant succession of hopeless incarnations (the samsara). Thus to be incarnated is a punishment; to desire rebirth, madness. True hope lies not in waiting for the ultimate, definitive, happy rebirth, but in renouncing it, in preventing it. Let us not deceive ourselves with images of metempsychosis, a succession of incarnations in other beings—in animals, plants, objects and then in men and women again. The cycle of rebirths can easily be applied to the individual's life: he constantly dies and is reborn, suffers but constantly hopes to be reborn in a new, happy life. Yet he encounters only pain.

All this incessant desiring, this searching and not finding, derives from the way we think of the world, from our concepts, primarily the concept of being. We cling to the idea that there is an ego, a soul, a world, a god, a class—which is to say an unambivalent state of love and a constant source of life. Eastern thought has radically rejected what is the original, immediate experience of the nascent state: "being is; nonbeing is not." By rejecting this initial problem, it has rejected all Western metaphysical thought, the source of our religion, philosophy and politics. The ideal of an objective absolute that is revealed to the rational animal moved by eros—the Greeks' reason—is basically a foolish hope in Hindu and Buddhist thought: a hope for a perpetually happy life, which is perpetually doomed to failure.

Passing from the language of philosophy to that of psychology, we can say that Eastern thought has developed another solution to the extreme depression in which the nascent state (and hence falling in love as well) originates. Instead of searching for a unique, unambivalent object of love that satisfies our desire, it tries to overcome desire; instead of seeking total passionate happiness, it tries to transcend happiness and pain: nirvana is this beatitude devoid of passion. What replaces the experience of falling in love, then, is an *ars erotica*, thanks to which we can receive pleasure from ourselves and from other people, but without depending on that unique, unmistakable other person who is different from all others and irreplaceable and whose loss means that everything is lost. This erotic wisdom also exploits individual inclinations, the preferences that everyone has, but it completely refuses to be tied to one person. Historically, this wisdom took the form of harems, the sexual communism of religious groups or religious prostitution. Such eroticism never claimed to be the basis for the conjugal couple and hence the family. In India as in China, the family was the product of the encounter between kinship systems, and so individual choice mattered little or not at all. The *ars erotica* was a way to derive pleasure from a relationship that in itself had no particular reason to give more satisfaction than another relationship. In the aristocratic classes where the *ars erotica* was developed, however, it was common practice to have concubines. In this way, sexuality was separated from marriage, from passion, even from affection for a single person.

In the West, the exact opposite has occurred: passionate eros has incorporated sexuality, mutual affection, marriage, even procreation. Only the West, only Europe, has tried to realize monogamy, has set it up as the ideal. Only Europeans have required, at a certain point, that the stability of the couple, the family, even the criteria for the perpetuation of the species be entrusted to the nascent state. What does it mean, in fact, to entrust to this state the choice of a spouse, a companion with whom we want to have a child? It means that we want to have a child with that person who, in our eyes, appears to be someone absolutely extraordinary, who has been judged entirely preferable to everyone else, in an absolute sense, and who has prepared us for a total struggle against all the rest. The incredible individualism of the West, the concept of the human being as something absolutely unique and endowed with value, is slowly constructed through the experience in which two people—each one extraordinary in the other's eyes—bring into the world what is extraordinary for both of them. All this is absent from the Eastern tradition: sexuality has found space for its extraordinary dimension in the *ars erotica*, but apart from any passion for the unique, irreplaceable individual. As a result, there is no falling in love, no pathological jealousy, no torment, no apathy, no nostalgia. Especially no nostalgia, that Western illness which makes us preserve in our hearts the marvelous image of a possibility that is already experienced or glimpsed in some way, and that perhaps—the day or hour is never mentioned—will throw open the doors to the happy age, the radiant dawn of the new day.

Since the postwar period, however, there has been a cultural exchange between the West and the East. On the one hand—above all, through Marxism—Western "hope" has entered Eastern countries as a systematic component of political thought and as a way of thinking. On the other hand, the Eastern suspicion of Western religious, political and personal absolutes has gained ground among ourselves as well. In the sphere of the couple, the principle of monogamous exclusivity in particular is increasingly criticized. The West has also absorbed participatory, collective forms of behavior and Eastern gnostic experiences that assure the attainment of a spiritual and erotic state by paths that differ from those for the individual who falls in love. Modern science itself has reached such a high degree of relativism that it completely rejects the concept of a thing in itself beyond the appearances revealed by instruments. Perhaps falling in love as a "recognized" form of behavior is on the decline. If so, this very book may be a sign of the transformation. Hegel said that thought, like the owl of Minerva, sees things only at sunset, discovers the meaning of a social phenomenon or institution only at the moment of its decline. It is very difficult to make predictions in this area. Certainly, in the history of the West, movements have been based on comprehensive ideologies, on the fervor of fanaticism and on intolerance. The critical analysis of movements and of the genesis of ideologies constitutes an essential program, a necessary undertaking in order to avoid future catastrophes. If this analysis should help to prevent new fanaticisms, it would certainly realize its historical task. And since falling in love basically has the same nature as collective movements, it too must be analyzed, studied, understood. Other paths must be explored, other institutions invented. The nascent state, as well as falling in love, will probably remain, and what will finally change will be only its cultural elaboration, its relationship to other social forms. I say this because, in general, a cultural tradition does not disappear; it is only reborn in other forms. Civilizations last for millennia, always.

ABOUT THE AUTHOR

FRANCESCO ALBERONI, who holds the chair of sociology at the University of Milan, was born in Piacenza in 1929. He has been studying the sociology of collective movements for nearly twenty years, and his book *Movement and Institution*, recently published in English translation by Columbia University Press, is considered a classic in its field. *Falling in Love* was a best seller in Italy and has been published with great success throughout Europe. Professor Alberoni also writes for Italy's leading newspaper, the *Corriere della Sera* of Milan, and for *Panorama*.

ABOUT THE TRANSLATOR

LAWRENCE VENUTI was born in Philadelphia. He received his Ph.D. degree from Columbia University in 1980 and is now assistant professor of English at Temple University. His articles and translations of Italian poetry and prose have appeared in many magazines and journals, including *Antaeus*, *Harper's*, *Modern Fiction Studies* and *Paris Review*. His most recent translation is *Restless Nights: Selected Stories of Dino Buzzati* (San Francisco: North Point Press, 1983).